A REASON FOR HOPE

A REASON FOR HOPE

The Human Experience
of the Kingdom of God

Adrian B. Smith

McCRIMMONS
Great Wakering   Essex

First published in 1986 by
McCrimmon Publishing Co Ltd
10–12 High Street   Great Wakering   Essex

© 1986 Adrian B Smith

ISBN   085597   390   0

Cover: Nick Snode

Typeset and printed in Hong Kong by
Permanent Typesetting & Printing Co Ltd

Contents

We can justly consider that the future of humanity lies in the hands of those who are strong enough to provide coming generations with reasons for living and hoping.

The World's Catholic Bishops,
Second Vatican Council, 1965,
(GS31).

References

Reference is made in the text to the following Second Vatican Council and papal documents:

AA = Vat II Decree on the Apostolate of the Laity.
AG = Vat II Decree on the Church's Missionary Activity.
DH = Vat II Declaration on Religious Freedom.
EN = Apostolic Exhortation of Pope Paul VI on Evangelisation in the Modern World, 1975.
GS = Vat II Constitution on the Church in the Modern World.
LG = Vat II Constitution on the Church.
NA = Vat II Declaration on the Relationship of the Church to Non-Christian Religions.
PP = Encyclical Letter of Pope Paul VI on the Development of Peoples, 1967.
UR = Vat II Decree on Ecumenism.

* * * *

Biblical quotations are from *The Good News Bible* unless otherwise stated.
JB = Jerusalem Bible

To the members of two organisations with whom I have been privileged to work during the last ten years—the *World Catholic Federation for the Biblical Apostolate* and *Movement for a Better World*—during which time my mind has been opened by them to the vast possibilities and exciting challenge for our times of the Good News of Jesus the Christ about our Father's Kingdom.

Foreword

The Second Vatican Council enriched our understanding of the Church by bringing into play many Scriptural images and by exploiting a variety of theological models. There is always a danger that we will narrow our vision by concentrating on one or other only, or confuse our understanding by sudden and disconnected shifts from one to another. Many images of the Church are at the same time images of the Kingdom, while others indicate that there is a distinction to be made. The Church is a focus for the Kingdom, both for its proclamation and its realisation. It does not mark out the limit of the Kingdom. The Church as herald, as servant, as sacrament looks beyond itself, and while it gives an open invitation to membership it is concerned to build up the Kingdom wherever by God's grace it has taken root. And the Kingdom will only and finally be brought to perfection by God's transcendent act.

Father Adrian Smith takes us simply and boldly through Scripture, tradition and history to fire us with zeal for the Kingdom. If he points up the contrasts between one age and another, or one understanding and another, it is in order to engage us in the work of building, and in a positive stance towards the world, which in spite of its sin is still a place of hope because the Spirit of Christ can set it free to grow into the Kingdom of God's creative and redeeming presence.

+ Francis Thomas

Bishop of Northampton

1. Whatever became of the Good News?

A very large number of people alive today, estimated at one fifth of the world's population, and found in almost every country, would claim that their philosophy of life is based on the teaching of a Jewish prophet named Jesus.

Jesus, who lived about two thousand years ago, was one of a number of wandering prophets in the small country of Palestine at that time, performing miracles and preaching of a new age to come. He was in the public eye for probably no longer than three years, before being condemned to death by the authorities for subversive activity. He never wrote anything himself but his teaching was recorded for posterity a generation later by a few of his followers. The thrust of his message—which he proclaimed as 'Good News' about an ideal Kingdom—was that a new age of the brotherhood of mankind was imminent, and in fact was a possibility already within the reach of everyone, if mankind was prepared to adopt the values of life and the way of relating to others that he lived himself. He never claimed to be divine but spoke of having his origin in God, and of his intimate union with God, which he promised was to be the destiny of all humanity too.

He chose a small band of disciples, whom he instructed to spread his message. They made the unique claim that a few days after his public execution he was seen by them to be alive. They claimed to have been given his spirit, and this fired them with zeal to proclaim that this man, Jesus of Nazareth, was not only the expected Messiah of the Jewish people but the Christ of all men, an incarnation of God.

As his followers grew in number and spread, and suffered persecution and re-emerged, the leaders had disagreements and factions appeared. During ensuing centuries there were struggles for power and splits in the leadership. Some groups denounced others as heretical, there was a watering down of the message by some and a return to the purity of the original message by others. From time to time alliances were formed between the leaders and different political and imperial powers. As the following assumed more organisation, more centralisation and more political involvement, and borrowed structures from different cultures—in particular the Roman Empire—it took on all the appearances of yet another great religion. With the need to retain control over Jesus' original message and to provide a rational justification for it, the message became increasingly philosophical and complex, to the point where most of the Christ's followers today have lost sight of its simplicity.

The present world crisis demands that we who are the heirs of that Good News return to listen again to that message as it was originally heard by and inspired new hope in the people of Galilee. Hope is a commodity particularly lacking today. The threat of extinction under which we all live, either instantaneously by a nuclear disaster or in the long run by our mismanagement of the earth's resources, is causing all of us, Christian and non-Christian alike, to share in a search for the way forward.

We who are Christian claim that the Good News of the Kingdom, as first announced by Jesus the Christ, is the message for our future, of the glorious destiny God envisages for mankind, for our whole cosmos. This is one reason why, after nearly 2,000 years, it is returning to the fore of the Church's proclamation, to the centre of her theology.

We see the Church, following the impetus given her 20 years ago by the deliberations of the Second Vatican Council, returning from a Church-centred to a Kingdom-centred paradigm, even to the extent that Pope Paul VI could declare in 1975:

'Only the Kingdom is absolute, and it makes everything else relative.' (EN 8)

A short statement with vast implications. This book sets out to explore some of those implications for our time.

There have been scores of erudite books written on the subject by theologians and biblical scholars

over the last couple of decades. I make no attempt
to compete with them, but I am grateful for the
spadework they have done. I write for the people I
meet in our parishes; people who are searching for
reasons for hoping.

To such it is offered, but with a warning. The
Kingdom message of Jesus is a radical message,
making great personal demands, which is why
perhaps after two thousand years it has still made
so little impact on our world. Perhaps hearing the
parables of the Kingdom read Sunday after Sunday
causes a familiarity which breeds the proverbial
contempt. The very word 'Kingdom' is not attrac-
tive to our ears, conjuring up in our minds feudal
images of those battles between kings which seem to
form so large a part of our history books.

Can we perhaps at least mentally replace it with a
contemporary term which recaptures the dynamic
of the original proclamation: the New Society, the
New Age, the World Society, God's blueprint for
the world? Each says something about Jesus' vision,
but not enough. We cannot, however, so easily
abandon the term 'Kingdom of God' since it is full
of biblical significance, and it is in the biblical context that the plan God has for us has been revealed.
Furthermore, we are trying to understand something that has a transcendental character, which
means that in this life we will never grasp its full
significance. But we can at least start upon our
exploration. I hope the reader will find it as exciting
as I have.

2. The roots of the Good News

To understand why Jesus expressed his teaching about the new age in terms of the Kingdom of God, we need to start by looking at the way the concept of God's kingship developed through the centuries of the Old Testament, and therefore what the expression meant to the people of Palestine brought up in this tradition as they listened to him.

There is the temptation, to which many biblical writers succumb, of trying to relate Jesus' ideas about the Kingdom to the ideas already in existence before his time. In doing so they miss the very newness of Jesus' message. Jesus said on one occasion:

> 'John (the Baptist) is greater than any man who has ever lived. But he who is least in the Kingdom of God is greater than John.' (Lk 7:28)

While acknowledging the Baptist's greatness, Jesus was declaring that he nevertheless belonged to an age that had passed. What was begun with Jesus was something radically new, of which the past had no equivalent. Although God's rule over his people is a recurrent theme of the Old Testament, the actual expression 'Kingdom of God', so frequently on the lips of Jesus, is not found as such in the Old Testament.

So this brief review of the development of thought in Old Testament times is not in order to explain the words of Jesus, but so that we may understand better the minds of the audience that heard them—and indeed why it frequently misconstrued them.

The Israelites were not the first people to name their god a king. A scripture scholar, Norman Perrin, wrote that among all peoples of the ancient Near East one finds a common myth[1] about a god who had created the world, who had overcome and slain the primeval monster and who continued to act as king to his people by annually renewing the fertility of the earth. The name for such a king varied from people to people. In Babylonia it was Marduk; in Assyria, Asshur; in Ammon, Milcom; in Tyre, Melkart; in Israel, Yahweh. Furthermore, each of these peoples regarded themselves as a 'chosen people', sustained by their god-king in their position in the world and protected by him against attack by other peoples. The Israelites had taken over the ancient myth from the Canaanites, who in turn had received it from the great kingdoms on the Euphrates, the Tigris and the Nile.

---

1. The word *myth* is used by scripture scholars, not as meaning a purely fictitious story, but as a complex of stories, some fact and some fantasy, which explain to a people the inner meaning of the universe and of human life.

Whereas neighbouring peoples had as well their human kings, the Israelites, until their settling in the Promised Land, had no such king. In designating Yahweh their king, they relied upon a God who journeyed with his people—'Emmanuel': God-with-us. Often in the Old Testament writings the terms king and creator have the same connotation (as in Ps 149:2) and the whole world is his throne (Pss 93, 47). Of special significance is the fact that as creator-king he preserves creation by being a just king (Pss 96, 97, 98, 99). Justice is a predominant theme of both Old and New Testaments.

Once the Israelites had changed their mode of life from that of a wandering tribe to a conquering and settled people and came more under the cultural influence of their neighbours, they began to clamour for a human king.

'Samuel was displeased with their request for a king; so he prayed to the Lord, and the Lord said, "Listen to everything the people say to you. You are not the one they have rejected; I am the one they have rejected as their king".' (I Sam 8:6–7)

The Israelites then had a series of kings up to the time of the Exile.

But even these kings were considered to be vice-roys of God. In David's address to the officials of Israel in Jerusalem, he says of God: 'He gave me many sons and out of them all he chose Solomon to rule over Israel, the Lord's Kingdom' (I Chron

28:5). And Nathan, conveying God's message to David about Solomon, says: 'I will put him in charge of my people and my kingdom forever' (I Chron 17:14).

As viceroys of God their role was not primarily to lead in battle, but to exercise justice, especially to those who needed it most. Jeremiah (22:3) describes what the Lord expected of his king:

> 'I, the Lord, command you to do what is just and right. Protect the person who is being cheated from the one who is cheating him. Do not ill-treat or oppress foreigners, orphans, or widows; and do not kill innocent people in this holy place.'

Their role was to serve their people, not to indulge in pomp or exercise power for their own aggrandizement. Jeremiah continues his instruction to King Jehoiakim, son of King Josiah:

> 'Doomed is the man who builds his house by injustice and enlarges it by dishonesty; who makes his countrymen work for nothing and does not pay their wages.' (22:13)

> 'Does it make you a better king if you build houses of cedar, finer than those of others? Your father enjoyed a full life. He was always just and fair.... He gave the poor a fair trial .... that is what it means to know the Lord.' (22:15–16)

During the 500 years following the Exile, the Jews had one long struggle for political freedom, and so the idea of God's Kingship began to take on revolutionary overtones, and this continued to be true in Jesus' own times. The expected coming of the Messiah was going to bring about a new era for the Hebrew people.

Since the Israelite expressed himself in material terms rather than in abstract ideas, salvation would come when God would make a revolutionary change in both man himself—removing the selfishness that opposed him to God's Law—and in the material situation: his crops would be blessed (Mic 4:1–5). It would be both a human and a cosmic salvation. God's Kingdom would be eternal, as Daniel says describing his vision: 'His authority would last forever, and his Kingdom would never end'; and it would be universal. 'He was given authority, honour and royal power, so that the people of all nations, races and languages would serve him' (Dan 7:14). This is echoed in Psalm 89: 'I will extend his Kingdom from the Mediterranean to the River Euphrates' (v 25): to the limits of the known world.

However, there were different expectations of the way in which this new, liberated era would come about. For the Pharisees the Kingdom would become a reality through the exact observance of the Law; for the Zealots a guerilla war would provoke God's intervention. It seems that the Essenes expected two Messiahs, one priestly and spiritual, the other kingly and political. So at the time of Jesus there was a variety of Messianic expectations. While we might say a Messiah as king and priest was the expectation of the intellectual groups (Essenes, Scribes and Pharisees), the ordinary people expected a prophet-judge. What was common to all parties was that the new Kingdom would be one of political freedom, since the integration of the political system and the Jewish religion was such that they believed political freedom was necessary in order to serve God. It was to people with these expectations that Jesus announced in the synagogue of Nazareth, taking to himself the words of Isaiah (61:1–2):

'The Spirit of the Lord is upon me, because he has chosen me to bring good news to the poor. He has sent me to proclaim liberty to the captives and recovery of sight to the blind; to set free the oppresséd and announce that the time has come when the Lord will save his people.'

To which he added:

'This passage of scripture has come true today, as you heard it being read.' (Lk 4:18–21)

3. Jesus manifests the Kingdom

While we are aware that the word Gospel means
Good News and is used to describe the message Jesus
brought mankind, there is a lot of confusion over
what the core of that Good News is. How do we
sum up in one phrase the central message of Jesus
which is supposed to have had such an impact on
his audience in Palestine and upon generations of
people since then? Ask any group of Christians
what, in a few words, this Good News is and one
gets as many different answers as there are people
present. Not that some answers are wrong and
others are right: they are really all different aspects
of the central theme of his teaching, which is about
the new age he is inaugurating, expressed in terms
of the Kingdom. Luke has Jesus say as much himself: 'I must preach the Good News of the Kingdom
of God ... because that is what God sent me to do'
(4:43).

When all the things Jesus said are heard in terms

of this central theme, the thrust of his Good News is a very simple message. Unfortunately, over the years and centuries conflicting interpretations of Scripture have been voiced. Those considered false have been countered very often by an over-stress of their opposite. With these different stresses on matters which are frequently peripheral to the central message, the thrust of that central message has been lost. The hundreds of theological works published each year, while of great interest to the scholar, can cause a bewildering maze in which the simplicity of Jesus' original message, and consequently the simplicity of Christian belief and Christian life, become quite obscured.

One particular obscurity with which we shall have to deal in a later chapter is the identifying of the Church with the Kingdom.

A consequence of our having lost the simplicity of Jesus' proclamation is that his Good News is not as exciting to people today as it was to those who heard it live from his lips in Galilee. Indeed we might ask whether it is even received as good news at all or whether, to some, it takes on the appearance of a burden to be assumed in this world as the price to pay for deliverance in the next. The announcement of God's wonderful liberating vision for mankind, God's initial plan for humanity, which is unfolding stage by stage through history, is not understood for what it is. In our present time, when we are more future-orientated than man has ever been before, and when our future looks so bleak to so many, we need more than ever to return to this central theme of Jesus. We need to understand not only how the

Kingdom is the only absolute value because it is what our world is all about, but how Jesus himself has raised mankind onto a higher plane of existence, the plane of the end time in which God's promises are drawing to fulfilment. Pope Paul VI emphasised the centrality of the Good News about the Kingdom when he wrote: 'As an evangeliser, Christ first of all proclaims a kingdom, the Kingdom of God; and this is so important that, by comparison, everything else becomes "the rest", which is "given in addition" (Mt 6:33). Only the Kingdom therefore is absolute, and it makes everything else relative' (EN 8).

But what, after all, is this Kingdom that Jesus is speaking about? It is clearly different from the Kingdom his listeners were expecting the Messiah to announce, just as he himself was a different kind of 'Saviour' from that expected at that time.

The picture will take some unravelling, because Jesus himself never defined the Kingdom in so many words. Remembering that the gospels and letters of the New Testament were written in Greek, it is interesting to note that the Greek word used by their authors for Kingdom is *basileia*, which is most literally translated as 'reign', and not 'realm' or 'domain'. It is not to be thought of as relating to a place. God reigns when his will is being lived. God's will is for the unfolding in created time of what St Paul refers to (Eph 1:9–10) as God's 'secret plan' which 'God will complete when the time is right'. But even if we can say that much, we are still left with the question of how we are to understand that 'secret plan', which is being worked out in our midst.

Before going further in our exploration, we need to clarify a confusion in our own time between three expressions that we find in Scripture: Kingdom of God, Kingdom of Heaven and Kingdom of Christ. The expression Kingdom of Christ and the implication that it is Christ's Kingdom rather than God's is not frequent. It is found only occasionally in the gospels (Lk 22:30, 23:42; Mt 13:41, 20:21, Jn 18:36) and would appear to be a notion that developed among the Apostles after Jesus' time. It is also mentioned five times in the epistles and once in the Book of Revelation. The probable explanation is that as the early Christians began to appreciate more that the Christ was invested with all the fullness of deity (Col 2:9) the term Christ and God became almost interchangeable. It is unlikely that Jesus himself ever spoke of the Kingdom as his Kingdom. Paul, as it were, decides the issue by explaining that at the end of time the Christ will hand over the Kingdom to God:

> 'Then the end will come; Christ will overcome all spiritual rulers, authorities and powers, and will hand over the Kingdom to God the Father... When all things have been placed under Christ's rule, then he himself, the Son, will place himself under God, who placed all things under him; and God will rule completely over all.' (I Cor 15:24–28)

When Mark and Luke record Jesus as using the phrase 'Kingdom of God', Matthew records the same sayings with the expression 'Kingdom of Heaven'. In fact, of the 46 times Matthew has Jesus speak of the Kingdom, only four times do we find the phrase 'Kingdom of God'. Since he was writing for Jewish Christians, he respects their custom of using a circumlocution in place of the holy name of God, just as we might exclaim 'Heaven help us' when we are really calling for God's help. Unfortunately, preachers in our own time do their congregations a disservice by using the term 'Kingdom of Heaven' as frequently as 'Kingdom of God' and thereby unwittingly cause it to be presented as a beyond-death reality.

Although John in his gospel uses the expression 'Kingdom' only twice—in Jesus' dialogue with Nicodemus (3:3, 5)—it is the most constantly recurring subject in the other three gospels, being mentioned 104 times, 91 times on the lips of Jesus: in Matthew 46 times, in Luke 31 times and in Mark 14 times. It is the subject of almost all the parables, of which 40 tell us what the Kingdom is like and 25 speak about the fate of those who are unprepared for the Kingdom.

Jesus communicated his oral message in two ways. A verse in Matthew's gospel distinguishes between his teaching and his preaching: 'Jesus went all over Galilee, teaching in the synagogues, preaching the Good News about the Kingdom' (4:23). His preaching is the announcement that the new and last age of the Kingdom has now arrived: his teaching is about the response that this event demands from us, the nature of the conversion that our acceptance of the Good News will bring about.

The preaching and the teaching are complementary aspects of his message.

Fortunately for us the Good News of the Kingdom is not confined to the realm of thoughts and beliefs. If it were, our holiness would depend on our erudition, our theological comprehension. It is about being raised to a new level of awareness which injects new life into our attitudes and our actions. It is an awareness of our potential and our possible relationship to God, of their availability to us right now, of our ability to live as sharers in the life of God. So it is available to professor and peasant alike.

It is a remarkable characteristic of Jesus' preaching and teaching that he was willing to share his message with anyone who would listen. It was not an academic teaching offered to a Scribal school trained in the Law of Moses, nor a secret teaching offered only to chosen initiates. Apart from Jerusalem he appears not to have taught in any of the major towns of Judea or Galilee, but confined himself to the obscure villages—in places such as Nazareth and Capernaum, which were obscure enough not even to obtain a mention in the Old Testament. Indeed, he himself gave a sign of his credentials to the inquiring disciples of John the Baptist that 'the Good News is preached to the poor' (Mt 11:5) as a fulfilment of the prophecy of Isaiah about the Messiah (Is 61:1).

Since the proclamation of the Kingdom was 'what God sent him to do', not only do we see it as the focal point of his preaching, but all the events and activities of his life centre upon this mission. His healing miracles, as we shall see in more detail later, were a sign of the presence of the Kingdom, both as a fulfilment of prophecy and as a conquering of the opposite forces, the forces of evil (Lk 11:20). His cosmic miracles, over the elements and material things, were the consequence of the power possessed by a fully developed man. His feasting and banquets were messianic signs that God's time of saving had come as well as being occasions for breaking down the social and cultural barriers between the 'clean' and 'unclean'. His re-casting of the Old Testament laws—'You have heard how it was said ... but I tell you ...' (Mt 5)—are a sign of the Kingdom person living at a deeper level of consciousness with greater sensitivity and awareness. His very passion and cruel death were a direct consequence of the non-acceptability of his message by those who felt their own authority and position to be threatened by him. His resurrection from death, and his entry into a new quality of life through the passage of death, were the consequence for the totally fulfilled man, (Rom 1:4), the man in whom the plan of God had become a reality.

4. The 'mystery' of the Kingdom

That the earth and the heavenly city penetrate each other is a fact accessible to faith alone. (GS 40)

Despite the fact that the Kingdom was the central point of Jesus' message, the proclamation of which was the purpose of his mission, we have no clear, defined idea of what he meant by the Kingdom. It remains, and to all on earth always will remain, a mystery. When we speak of a religious concept or event as a mystery, we are not saying we cannot apprehend it. We are saying that because it contains a divine element it has a greater dimension than we are able to understand by reason. To define something is to confine it: to put it within parameters which enable us to contain it, to control it, to give it limits. We cannot box in anything which has a divine element. To do so would be to confine God and to reduce him to our mental limitations.

The Greek word for 'mystery' is *mysterion*, meaning a knowledge someone can acquire, not through an educational process, by inductive and deductive reasoning—the channel of exterior revelation—but only through experience and insight—God revealing Truth through intuitive knowledge.

The Kingdom is not limited to a place, nor to an event. It is a symbol of the destiny God has designed for mankind—something we are always striving towards which cannot be grasped by us with our present limited consciousness. We need such symbols of the perfect future to compel us onwards just as the Israelites while wandering in the arid desert before entering the 'Promised Land' encouraged each other with a description of a perfect, well-watered, fertile garden of plenty where all was harmony and where man and woman walked with God in bliss. This was the symbol of what God really intended for all humanity, and they called it Eden.

We attain a comprehension of the Kingdom not by hearing about it but by experiencing it. And we experience it by living according to its values, which is only possible after we have been through a conversion process which is so radical that it is called a rebirth. In the womb our eyes are closed, our world is minimal. At birth we have such a new experience that we enter a new level of consciousness: we see, we hear, we feel, we smell, we taste. We begin to 'know' our world; that is, to be aware of it, to interpret it. So great is the conversion to Kingdom awareness that Jesus uses this example of birth with Nicodemus:

'I am telling you the truth: no one can see the

Kingdom of God unless he is born again' (John 3:3). 'No one can enter the Kingdom of God unless he is born of water and the Spirit' (v 5).

Nicodemus was mystified by this, as well he might have been. 'How can a grown man be born again?' he asks. In fact the Greek word translated as 'again' can also be rendered as 'from above'.

The life of the Kingdom is so new, demanding such a change of personality, that it can come to us only as God's gift. Some spiritual writers have interpreted Jesus' mention of water here to mean that such enlightenment comes only through Baptism, and is in consequence the prerogative of Christians. But water is symbolic of the fullness of life which comes from the cleansing power of the Spirit. Jesus goes on to say 'You must *all* be born again' (v 7), but not all in fact receive sacramental baptism.

In speaking about the Kingdom, Jesus was at a further disadvantage in that his Jewish listeners were interpreting what he was saying in the light of their expectations of a future political kingdom. He had not come to preach Jewish nationalism; he never spoke against their Roman oppressors. He had not come to restore the glorious kingdom of David, though many understood his message this way (Mk 11:10) and even his own disciples were expecting it, as was expressed in the disappointment of two of his followers walking to Emmaus after his death: 'We had hoped that he would be the one who was going to set Israel free' (Lk 24:21). The Kingdom he announced was not purely spiritual, but nor could it be reduced simply to politics.

The majority of Jesus' Kingdom sayings are descriptive of the Kingdom rather than proclaiming it; and, being unable to define it, they come across with an air of mystery. For the ordinary people he had to use the symbolic language of the parable. To his disciples alone could he make the notion more explicit: 'The knowledge of the secrets of the Kingdom of God has been given to you, but to the rest it comes by means of parables' (Lk 8:10).

Even so, right up to the last moment of their earthly contact with Jesus, at the moment of his Ascension, they asked him: 'Lord will you at this time give the Kingdom back to Israel?' (Acts 1:6). It would take their enlightment by the Spirit at Pentecost to enable them to reflect back on their years in the company of Jesus and perceive in it the full meaning of the Christ event.

Another aspect of the Kingdom which gives it an element of mystery, and one which continues to cause biblical scholars to write an endless number of explanatory papers, is the tension between the 'now' but 'not yet' of its fulfilment. Jewish writers before Jesus' time predicted that the Kingdom would come about as a great catastrophic, apocalyptic event, external to humanity. Although a few of Jesus' Kingdom sayings refer to the future (as in the Lord's Prayer) none of them is apocalyptic. Jesus sees, rather, the Kingdom coming to fulfilment from within a person, a powerful energy, already present and released through Jesus' own ministry. However, it can only be fully understood by us when we are part of and party to its fulfilment, which will happen beyond time. We could too easily excuse ourselves from any co-operation with God's plan by saying it will be fulfilled only 'at the end of time'. True, it is God's Kingdom, he alone empowers it to become a reality, but he chooses to involve us in bringing it about. Otherwise Jesus' instruction to his disciples to pray for its coming, 'Thy Kingdom come' (Mt 6:10), would be a charade. No, the end time happens when mankind has taken Jesus' formula for life sufficiently seriously that the Kingdom has become a reality, it has grown through time. It will be the moment when there becomes on earth that reality so beautifully described in the words of the Preface for the feast of Christ the King: 'An eternal and universal kingdom: a kingdom of truth and life, a kingdom of holiness and grace, a kingdom of justice, love and peace.' This double aspect of the Kingdom—as a reality of the present while being a reality of the future—is apparent in some of the parables in Matthew's gospel. For instance, chapter 13 (the sower, the weeds, the mustard seed, the yeast, the hidden treasure, the pearl, the net,) as well as in others of his parables: the unforgiving servant (18:23–35), the workers in the vineyard (20:1–16), the ten virgins (25:1–13).

Using the imagery of the parable of the treasure hidden in the field, we could tell it this way: God has already donated us a field, quite gratuitiously, and he has made it known that the supreme treasure is buried there. So now we are in possession of that field but we are still trying to discover the treasure: we have not taken possession of the treasure, not yet claimed it.

This aspect of the mystery of the Kingdom becomes easier to understand when we regard its fulfilment as the fulfilment of the eternal plan God has for mankind, indeed had since the beginning of time. In the eternal NOW of God, outside our creation-limitation of time, the Kingdom exists in its fullness because it is the fulfilment of God's plan which cannot be other than successful. In its working out, however, in the context of created time, it has its advances and its setbacks—it is incomplete—and is dependent for its working out in the time element upon mankind's free co-operation with God. Within its being worked out in time, there are moments when it takes a great leap forward.

The coming of the Christ into our world caused the whole of humanity to take just such a great evolutionary leap towards our final destiny. One element of this forward leap is that Jesus revealed to us that there is indeed a plan. Paul writes of this to the Church in Ephesus:

> 'God did what he had purposed, and made known to us the secret plan he had already decided to complete by means of Christ. This plan, which God will complete when the time is right, is to bring all creation together, every-thing in heaven and on earth, with Christ as head'. (1:9–10)

We find in this passage one of the phrases which is key to understanding the nature of the Kingdom: 'to bring all creation together'. It includes the aspects both of the unity of the whole of humanity in God and of the cosmic dimension of the plan.

So Jesus was not able to give us any real formula to tell us exactly what is meant by the phrase 'the

Kingdom of God'. He could only present us with the ingredients of a composite picture which, under the guidance of his Spirit, we have to put together. This collage is made up partly of parables, which of their nature are open-ended, non-defining, non-confining, having something to say to each person according to his level of awareness. It is made up partly of Jesus' 'Magna Carta' of the Kingdom (the Sermon on the Mount, Mt 5–7); partly of his own way of life and the values he lived by: his sitting at table with sinners (Mk 2:15–17), his attitude towards lepers (Mt 8:3), towards adulterers (Jn 8:3–11), towards tax-collectors (Lk 19:1–9), and towards other of society's outcasts (Jn 4:5–41). His miracles, too, which were themselves intended to be vehicles of the message, contribute to the overall picture. When John the Baptist's disciples were looking for a straight answer to their question: 'Are you he who is to come, or should we expect someone else?' he referred them for an answer to his 'signs': 'Go back and tell John what you have seen and heard: the blind see again, the lame walk, lepers are cleansed, and the deaf hear, the dead are raised to life, the Good News is proclaimed to the poor' (Lk 7:22–23, *JB*).

For those who were well disposed—'those who had ears to hear and eyes to see'—the signs were there to be seen: signs that a Messiah had come into their midst, that a new age had dawned. 'During his stay in Jerusalem for the Passover many believed in his name when they saw the signs that he gave' (Jn 2:23, *JB*).

But it was above all in his own person that the

Kingdom was manifest, so that Mark could open his gospel declaring that the Good News is about Jesus: 'This is the Good News about Jesus Christ, the son of God' (Mk 1:1). This deserves a chapter on its own.

5. Jesus, the Kingdom Person

This is not the place to present yet another life of Jesus. But since both his style of life and the values by which he lived illustrate what he was preaching as well as being the cause of its coming about, it is necessary to highlight certain aspects of his life so that our future reading of the gospels can be from this Kingdom perspective.

The Second Vatican Council decree on the nature of the Church reminds us that: 'In Christ's *word*, in his *works*, and in his *presence* this Kingdom reveals itself to men... The *miracles* of Jesus also confirm that the Kingdom has already arrived on earth... Before all things, however, the Kingdom is clearly visible in the *very person* of Christ, Son of God and Son of Man ...' (LG5, italics mine).

We must always keep in mind while reading the four gospels that the evangelists were not taking down a dictation of Jesus' words at the time he spoke them, but writing many years after the event, with the hindsight given them by the inspiration of the Spirit at Pentecost; and writing for particular groups of Christians with different backgrounds. The probable reason why the main thrust of the apostles' preaching was about the person of Jesus as the centre of the Good News, rather than about the Kingdom—the expression 'the Kingdom of God' appears only seven times in the Acts of the Apostles, mostly in reporting Paul's preaching—was that, while the term had great historical significance for the Jews, it would have meant little to Greek-culture Christians. Therefore the Apostles did not hesitate to identify the person of Jesus with the Good News and the Kingdom. For instance, where Luke quotes Jesus as saying: 'I assure you that anyone who leaves home or wife or brothers or parents or children for the sake of the Kingdom of God will receive much more in this present age ...' (Lk 18:29), Mark quotes '... for me and for the gospel ...' (Mk 10:29).

In John's gospel, written very much later than the other three—perhaps as much as 60 years after the Resurrection—and from quite a different perspective, the identification of the Kingdom with Jesus is even more explicit. In fact, as we have already mentioned, the word only occurs twice in this gospel, both times in Jesus' dialogue with Nicodemus (3:3 and 5), apart from Jesus referring to 'my kingdom' in his few words with Pilate, on which occasion he describes his mission in these words: 'I was born and came into the world for this one purpose, to speak about the truth' (18:36, 37). The implication is that it is only through accepting the truth of his announcement of the Kingdom, only through faith in him as the one who makes the

Kingdom a reality, does the Kingdom become a reality in our lives.

While the other three evangelists have Jesus declare his message in terms of the Kingdom, John has him declare it in terms of 'life', the fullness of life. That, for John, is what the Kingdom is about. God's plan for mankind is that we should all attain fullness of life—the fullness of our humanity—in union with God. The word 'life' or 'eternal life' occurs in John 36 times, and he recounts Jesus as saying: 'I have come in order that you might have life—life in all its fullness' (Jn 10:10). Jesus understands himself to be the channel of God's life to mankind; and our means to receive this life already now in its fullness is to accept Jesus and his message. 'Anyone who believes in the Son has eternal life, but anyone who refuses to believe in the Son will never see life' (Jn 3:36, *JB*). Thus it is not only Jesus and the Kingdom John identifies, but both in turn are related to Eternal Life.

While Jesus himself proclaimed the Kingdom, the early Church of the apostles proclaimed Jesus. And yet it is abundantly clear from the accounts of Jesus they give us in the gospels that Jesus did not ask his disciples to rally round his person as an object of cult or respect. Indeed, unlike the prophets before him, and unlike the gurus of other religions, whose followers were made up of those who gathered round them voluntarily and not by call, Jesus deliberately chose 'the Twelve'. With his vision of the Kingdom as a new age that was intended to grow ever outwards from its tiny beginning (the mustard seed), he needed a group to continue his mission after him. The choice of men he made, therefore, is instructive. Since he was not founding a new religion or a new institution, he did not require men who could assimilate and then proclaim convincingly a new doctrine, nor men possessing organisational ability. He required men who were open enough to be touched by the radical nature of his message, men who would be fired with enthusiasm because they had experienced in his company a new way of living, a new attitude to religious values, a new appreciation of the worth of each human person, and above all, a new way of relating to God through an intimate child-parent relationship.

This last point, of Jesus introducing mankind to a quite new relationship with God, needs special emphasis because it is really the key to understanding what was so new in Jesus' message and why its acceptance causes us to make a quantum leap towards our final goal, which we call the fullness of the Kingdom.

It is true that we find God referred to as a father of the nation in Old Testament writings, but the title is used to indicate God's care for his people as creator, the supplier of their needs, the winner of their battles. Jesus uses the title with an entirely different meaning and value, with affection. It was a shift from a father-of-the-tribe experience to a father-of-each-individual-person experience. And that required an immense psychological development.

Jesus understood himself to be chosen to live in a quite personal relationship to God: 'The Father chose me and sent me into the world' (Jn 10:36).

His mission was centred on the absolute power of God operating through him. All the good he did was attributed to God, whereas he was extremely reserved in speaking about himself. So passionately had he identified God's cause with his own that he was able to heal (Lk 9:42–43) and to forgive sin in his own name (Lk 5:20–21). Nowhere is his unique relationship with God more clear than in the way he addresses God and speaks of God as his father in that intimate family term 'Abba', an Aramaic word which is probably the most historically correct and authentic word we have of Jesus. Jesus is recorded as using the expression '*my* father' 46 times. Indeed, such is his obsession with his father that there are few pages of the gospels that do not carry some reference to him.

Since such intimacy with God was in stark contrast with the current way of relating to God, it seems to have been noted by the evangelists as quite special to Jesus and as expressing the central point of his spirituality. 'I am in the Father and the Father is in me' (Jn 14:11). It led to his fellow villagers from Nazareth being scandalised by him: who does he think he is, this carpenter, this son of Mary whose brothers are James, Joseph, Judas and Simon? They rejected him (Mk 6:1–3). It would eventually lead him to the cross on a charge of blasphemy: 'You are only a man, but you are trying to make yourself God' (Jn 10:33).

This new relationship between God and man, understood and lived by Jesus, and offered to all mankind through Jesus—'No one goes to the Father except by me' (Jn 14:6)—is, with its consequence, the fundamental characteristic of his new age. The consequence is that, accepting a common father, we must accept to love and treat every other human being as our brother and sister whatever our difference in culture, national loyalty or religious persuasion. This provides the formula for a new world indeed. It is the only explanation for the openness of Jesus to all people, without exception, cutting through all the barriers the law and custom had set up. Paul glimpsed the wonder of this vision: '... there is no longer any distinction between Gentiles and Jews, circumcised and uncircumcised, barbarians, savages, slaves, and free men, but Christ is all, Christ is in all' (Col 3:11). It is, however, so new, so radical, so unbelievably utopian, that even after 2,000 years since this breakthrough there are few signs that the invitation is being taken very seriously. Even today we, his declared followers, have great difficulty in turning from an Old Testament God 'out there' to feel comfortable with a God with whom we can relate intimately and with affection. We will return to a practical application of this immense revelation in the last chapter.

In carrying mankind to the fullness of life, Jesus saw himself battling with all forms of negativity. In the language of his time and his environment, he expressed this as a battle between two kingdoms: the reign or power of God overcoming the reign of Satan. The stage was set early in his life in the scene described as the Temptations in the Desert. He saw all aspects of his mission as a fight against evil. When the 72 disciples returned from their mission they reported: 'Lord, even the demons obeyed us when we gave them a command in your name' And he replied: 'I saw Satan fall like lightning from heaven' (Lk 10:17–18). His saving task was to be a liberating from all that is bad, oppressive, alienating, impoverishing. His saving power is a power that makes whole, that makes us fully human, that gives 'life in abundance'. Perhaps no account of Jesus' healing ministry better demonstrates his power to make whole and better describes, in a language loaded with symbolism, the divisive power of evil, than that of his casting the 'unclean spirit' out of the man in the territory of the Gerasenes, (Mk 5:1–20). The man is described as living 'among the tombs': he is not only ritually unclean but associated with death and decay. He is quite uncontrollable and of astonishing strength; no amount of chains and irons could hold him: the strength of evil power is not to be underestimated. His 'wandering through the hills, screaming and cutting himself with stones' tell of his disorientation, and the self-destructive nature of evil. He is no longer an integrated person—'My name is Legion'—but disintegrated enough to take possession of 2,000 pigs. Jesus' healing strength restored his wholeness, holiness and self-respect: we are told 'he was sitting there clothed and in his right mind'.

The new relationship with God that Jesus opened up to us is not oppressive but intimate, one in which man is no longer oppressed by a sabbath law. His forgiveness of sins is an obvious aspect of his liberating action, and in a cultural context which was particularly prone to see any kind of suffering as being the consequence of sin (Jn 9:2), he dedicated himself especially to seek out the sinners: 'I did not come to call the virtuous, but sinners' (Mk 2:17, *JB*). The Judaism of Jesus' time, unlike classical Judaism, was particularly preoccupied with the influence of demons—which may be why the Christian tradition seemed to be over concerned with Satan and his devils for so many centuries—such that the suffering of the blind, the deaf, the dumb, the epileptic was attributed to evil spirits. Jesus' miracles of physical healing, therefore, were not a presentation of his credentials as a man of God, not done to win fame—on the contrary, he often insists that news of his miracles is not spread (Mk 5:43)—but works of victory of God's Kingdom over that of the Evil One. His bringing dead people back to life, his curing leprosy and paralysis, were likewise a liberating of people from some form of bondage to make them whole. They were a proclamation of his message in action.

His acts of breaking down the cultural and social barriers, seen particularly in his eating habits, were also done to heal the divisions between different groups of people. On one occasion he will eat with sinners and publicans (Lk 15:2). On another he will accept the table hospitality of the Pharisees (Lk 7:36–50). This is particularly significant when we remember that the banquet was a way of describing the fulfilment of the Kingdom in the Old Testament prophecies. It was on the occasion of banquets that Jesus delivered some of his most beautiful parables.

Jesus' varied acts to overthrow the demoniac power structure should not obscure from our view just how creative and up-building and positive his mission and his message was. He was concerned to 'make all things new' and so many of his parables are about growth (see all those in Mt 13 and Mark 4). One aspect of the positive, creative character of his mission is the universality of his message. It is not a judgement of vengeance on sinners and god-less men, as many of Jesus' contemporaries understood the coming Kingdom to be (eg the Qumran community and John the Baptist) but a healing, saving message of peace and joy. It is significant that when Jesus declares his manifesto in the synagogue of Nazareth, at the beginning of his public life (Lk 4:16–19), he does so by quoting Isaiah (61:1–2) which describes the coming of God's Kingdom, and he concludes with the words 'the time has come when the Lord will save his people' but omits to add the following line from Isaiah, 'and defeat their enemies'. There is to be no more division between a Chosen People and their enemies. What is going to be decisive for salvation is not membership of Israel but conversion—a change from a self-orientated life to a life given to and for others.

Jesus made the new age—what Pope Paul describes as 'the new world, the new state of things, the new manner of being, of living, of living in community, which the Gospel inaugurates' (EN 23)—a reality precisely by living as a new-age person. By living and by relating to people as if the new age had already come, not with a 'let's pretend' approach but with the conviction that with and through him it actually had come, and by his very living of these new-age values, he *did* make it a reality and this was why he was recognised as having a different kind of authority from the Scribes (Mt 7:29). And the Scribes at the time had considerable authority. They were one of the three dominant classes of Jewish society, rivalling the priestly aristocracy (the 'chief priests') and the lay nobility (the 'elders'). Their influence derived not from their birth nor from their wealth but from their learning. The authority of Jesus was of a quite different kind: it lay in the authenticity of his message (Lk 4:22), which was recognisable to all of good will. While the Scribes' authority was a legal, institutionalised authority, that of Jesus derived from his own personal charism. He frequently appeals for faith from his listeners, but it is not for faith in God nor for faith in his own divinity but for faith in himself as the Messiah, as the one who ushers in the new age. It is a plea to share in his own belief that the new age comes about by being lived. The same plea is made to his followers in every age as it is today: the new age will become a reality, the end time will be reached, when we can take the great leap forward into an entirely new manner of living, regulating our lives by the values he gives us.

6. The dimensions of the Kingdom

On account of the identification of the Kingdom with the Church for so many centuries, a question often arises about membership of the Kingdom. The very question reveals an institutional notion of the Kingdom, whereas the Kingdom is not so much an entity as an experience, an experience of God's reign, God's blueprint for mankind breaking into our consciousness and dictating our manner of living.

Jesus had this experience to so profound a degree that it was a reality to him and became a reality for the world through him. The prayer he taught us to say for the coming of the Kingdom includes the wish that 'thy will be done' (according to Matthew's version) following on immediately from 'thy kingdom come'. In other words, a plea that God's plan be actualised already now in our midst: 'on earth as it is heaven'.

We notice that Jesus never described anyone as being *in* the Kingdom, which might have had the implication that some were outside the Kingdom, although 25 of his 65 Kingdom parables are about the fate of those who are unprepared for the Kingdom. He did, however, tell the lawyer who quizzed him about the greatest commandment: 'You are not far from the Kingdom of God' (Mk 12:34). The lawyer was nearing the point of experiencing the Kingdom because he had the right understanding about the priority of loving God and neighbour over the offering of animals and sacrifices to God.

Years later, St Paul was to become very impatient with the petty squabbles among the Christians in Rome as to which kind of food was ritually clean and which unclean. He had to remind them that 'God's Kingdom is not a matter of eating and drinking, but of the righteousness, peace and joy which the Holy Spirit gives' (Rom 14:17). 'Righteousness' is a word that sounds somewhat pompous to our ears today. It was current in the Old Testament world to refer to keeping ritual observances, which is why, perhaps, we very rarely find it used by Jesus: Matthew is the only one who puts this word on Jesus' lips. In the New Testament context, as Paul uses it here, it is better understood as 'right relationships', the fruits of which are peace and joy. The righteousness of Jesus is love for others. In I Cor 6:9, Paul announces that the unrighteous will not possess God's Kingdom, and he goes on in the next verse to give a list of such—'people who are immoral or who worship idols or are adulterers or homosexual perverts or who steal or are greedy or are drunkards or who slander others or are thieves—none of these will possess God's Kingdom'. All these people have one thing in common: they are non-relating persons, self-centred persons.

There are two points Paul is making in his admonition to the Romans. The first is that the Kingdom is not furthered by the observance of laws and regulations (the old form of righteousness) but by our right relationships, which is an entirely new mode of living.

The second point he makes is that this new way of living is the fruit of the Holy Spirit. As God's will for mankind, it is God's gift to mankind; not something that we can bring about by our own effort. As a dream for our future it is as utopian as the Marxist dream, and is just as concerned with mankind's relationship to this earth's goods, but differs essentially in the way it is to come about. It is not a human product but God's.

Jesus' parable about the growth of the seed has a lot to tell us of God's part and our part in the processes of making the Kingdom a reality:

> 'A man scatters seed in his field. He sleeps at night, is up and about during the day, and all the while the seeds are sprouting and growing. Yet he does not know how it happens. The soil itself makes the plants grow and bear fruit; first the tender stalk appears, then the ear, and finally the ear full of corn. When the corn is ripe, the man starts cutting it with his sickle, because harvest time has come'. (Mk 4:26–29)

The seed once planted grows with an inevitability and according to a pattern predetermined by the species of seed. It is God who gives the growth, not us. Nevertheless, to bring the process to its finale our co-operation is asked for, to sow the seed in the first instance (and no doubt to fertilise and weed during the growth), then to harvest at the right moment. But our part in the growth of the Kingdom is no more than co-operative. Our co-operation hastens its fulfilment. So Peter writes in his second letter: 'Do your best to make it come soon' (2 Pet 3:12).

This is why Jesus never told us to build the Kingdom, but he did invite us to enter it (Mk 10:15, 23–25). Perhaps this is better translated as to enter into: to enter into its spirit, to be possessed by it, to be born again. Paul explains: 'Your hearts and minds must be made completely new, and you must put on the new self, which is created in God's likeness and reveals itself in the true life that is upright and holy' (Eph 4:23–24). Only by entering into the spirit of it does it take hold of you. Only by starting to swim do we get the feel of swimming and so learn to swim; no amount of telling us about it turns us into swimmers. By living it we become 'actualisers' of the Kingdom. Like the seed, it grows outwards from within.

Are there, then, those who do not enter into the Kingdom way of life? Are they excluded from the Kingdom? What of the millions who have never had the chance to hear the Good News of Jesus the Christ?

When we consider the Kingdom in its plenitude as the accomplishment of God's plan for the fulfilment of each person within the unity of mankind, and indeed of the whole cosmos, then it is clear that everyone born into this world is potentially a 'member', a part, of God's Kingdom, whether conscious of that destiny or not. God's designs would be frustrated if every single person were not offered, in mysterious ways known only to God, the opportunity of full participation in the Kingdom, of 'reaching to the very height of Christ's full stature' (Eph 4:13), certainly in the next life, but even to some degree in this.

The phrase 'participation in the Kingdom' can mean two things. It can mean living with a consciousness of our wonderful destiny and of what Jesus has revealed to us about it, and so living our lives as a response to this invitation, as Kingdom people. By living by the values of the Kingdom one is actively, and even purposefully, making the Kingdom a reality in this present time.

But they also 'participate' in the furthering of God's plan, even quite unconsciously, who by any deed contribute to the uniting of mankind and to personal growth towards full humanity. Let me give two examples of this.

While I was living in Zambia, thousands of atheist labourers from mainland China worked for several years to build a railway from the coast of Tanzania into Zambia. They would have been astonished to be told they were furthering the Kingdom of God in that part of the world. Nothing would have been more remote from their intention. But in fact, by opening up great areas of both countries by this new form of communication, that is just what they were doing: they were improving the quality of life of thousands of peasant farmers, enabling them to live lives which are more fully human, and therefore more in conformity with God's plan for them.

The greatest Kingdom-promoting events the world has ever known have happened very recently. They were inspired not by the United Nations, nor by any joint action of the Christian Churches or world religions. They were the inspiration of a member of a, till then, little known pop music group, the Boomtown Rats. Urged by the need to raise money for the starving millions of Africa, Bob Geldof organised first a mammoth concert, Live Aid, concurrently in London and Philadelphia, lasting 16 hours and watched by an estimated 1,500,000,000 people in 160 countries, breaking all television audience records. That was on July 13, 1985. On May 25, 1986, this was followed by an even more all-encompassing event, Sport Aid. Watched by the same mass TV audience, 30,000,000 people in 272 cities across 78 countries ran a sponsored 10 km, not to mention participation in every other conceivable form of sport, in an act of solidarity with the destitute in Africa. Why do I call these Kingdom-promoting events? Never before, in the whole history of mankind, have so many people been united across all barriers of language, culture, ideologies and religions, in 160 countries in one common action, and that to raise money (£50 million in the case of Live Aid) for the deprived. In terms of St Paul's description of God's plan—the unification of all creation (Eph 1:10)—this was indeed a great religious act. 'What God the Father considers to be pure and genuine religion is this: to take care of orphans and widows in their suffering ...' (James 1:27).

These are one-off events. But there is in the world a minority group of 'professionals' made up of those who have pledged themselves to a lifelong commitment to live by and to be a witness to the values Jesus preached, for the sake of furthering the Kingdom vision. This group, calling itself the Church, has been described by the participants of the Second Vatican Council in these words:

> 'The Church ... receives the mission to proclaim and establish among all peoples the kingdom of Christ and of God. She becomes on earth the initial budding forth of that kingdom... The Church strains toward the consummation of the kingdom ...' (LG 5)

The Church has been entrusted with the task of continuing in each age the proclamation of the Good News of Jesus; of revealing the wonderful things God is doing in his world, as Jesus explained them to us. This revelation is available only to those to whom it is offered, and the channel through which it is offered is the Church. To say that where the Church is not present this revelation is not available (Rom 10:14–15) is not at all the same thing as saying that those who are not Christians are not also, in some mysterious way, graced to make their contribution to the coming of the Kingdom, as we have seen with the Chinese railway builders above.

Various attempts have been made to explain how this can be. The German theologian Karl Rahner coined the expression 'Anonymous Christians' to describe those who under, but unaware of, Christ's influence are agents of the Kingdom. It is an unhappy expression, not only because it is offensive to members of other religions—we would not like the Hindus to call us anonymous Hindus—but because to be a Christian means to be a disciple of Christ, and one cannot be a follower of Christ without expressing that commitment through membership of Christ's community, the Church. Any person may act 'christianly', that is according to the values of Christ; but that is quite different from making a commitment to continue Christ's mission to the world, which commitment is made through the sacrament of Baptism in which one acknowledges Christ as Lord of one's life and vows to convert oneself to live by his standards. Perhaps such persons would be better described as 'anonymous Kingdom participants', their participation varying with their degree of being, even unconsciously, contributors to the making-present of the Kingdom.

If we acknowledge, as we must, that there is some goodness in every human being, as persons created in the image of God, then we acknowledge that there are moments in the lives of even the apparently most wicked people when some expression of altruistic love, some kindly deed, furthers the coming of the Kingdom. The point that Rahner was wanting to make was that all such deeds, done consciously or not, as furthering the Kingdom, are done only because all mankind has been empowered by Christ who was 'the first among many brothers' (Rom 8:29).

An African theologian, Laurenti Magesa, prefers

the expression 'The New People of God'. Just as in the Old Testament the 'People of God' were the small percentage of mankind of one race (the Israelites) who were graced by God to prepare mankind for the moment when God would live among us in the person of Jesus, so the New People of God, of our own New Testament times, are made up of all people, world-wide, who co-operate with God's creative plan, the Kingdom. They are the unifiers of mankind who form a fellowship through their common intention, albeit an invisible fellowship. They are inspired by an inner convicton which is not necessarily expressed in Christian terms.

Some of these New People of God commit themselves to witness to God's Kingdom within the visible community called Church. On the other hand, not all who would call themselves Church members are part of the New People of God, because for some their Church membership is no more than a sociological fact which came about by their baptism as infants, but they have never been required to make an explicit profession of their commitment. Their membership has not led to their acquiring an inner conviction of their calling to promote the unity of mankind.[1]

There are two further dimensions of the Kingdom revealed by Jesus which complement each other. The Kingdom has a social dimension: it is

1. The reader will notice we are deliberately not looking at these questions in terms of who is 'saved' and who is not 'saved', on account of the variety of meanings attached to the word.

about the way people relate to each other—and this after all is what we shall be judged upon (Mt 25:31–46)—and it is all about the unity of all mankind with Christ as head (Eph 1:10). But at the same time it has a personal, interior dimension which calls for a conversion of our personal attitudes and our scale of moral values. This raises the question of whether the Kingdom is primarily an exterior, sociological phenomenon or an interior, spiritual reality. Both views have found their supporters since the time of Jesus.

At the heart of the debate, from the early Fathers of the Church to present-day Scripture scholars, is the Greek word *entos* which is used in a reply by Jesus, quoted only in Luke (17:20–21):

> 'Some Pharisees asked Jesus when the King-dom of God would come. His answer was, "The Kingdom of God does not come in such a way as to be seen. No one will say 'Look, here it is!' or, 'There it is!', because the Kingdom of God is *entos* you" ...'

The word *entos* can be translated either as 'within' you or as 'among' you, 'in your midst'[2]. Let us accept the ambiguity as indicating that both inter-pretations provide us with essential dimensions of

---

2. There are those who would argue from the context that the social meaning is the correct interpretation because Jesus was answering a question posed to him by the Pharisees—surely the least likely people to be told that they had the right inner dispositions of the Kingdom—and the answer he gave is to a question about *when* the Kingdom would come, for which the latter meaning is ▷

the Kingdom. We will first see what is meant by the Kingdom as an inner, spiritual reality.

To enter into the fullness of the Kingdom, to become a conscious promoter of the Kingdom, it is not sufficient to know about it. Jesus did not come simply to impart information. Paul reminds us: 'The Kingdom of God is not a matter of words, but of power' (I Cor 4:20). He came to challenge us to become a new people, to be born again into the fullness of life. There is one word which keeps appearing in his announcement of the presence of the Kingdom: 'conversion' or 'repentance'.

When we meet expressions like 'repent' or 'turn away from your sins' (Mk 1:15), we might understand them as 'be sorry for your sins'. In the Greek language, in which the gospels were written, they are a much more forceful expression, demanding a radical change of one's basic values, an about-turn, a con-version, indeed a new beginning, a 'rebirth' without which one cannot enter the Kingdom (Jn 3:3) In announcing the Kingdom, Jesus challenged, indeed reversed, the scale of values, the judgements, the attitudes of his contemporaries. In the Kingdom:

> The lowly are exalted and the mighty brought down. (Lk 1:52)

▷ the more likely answer. Other scholars counter this argument by saying that in the oral tradition Jesus' saying had an independent existence and that Luke decided to record it in the context of the Pharisees' question. The traditional translation of the Greek word *entos*, however, is 'within'.

The poor, the children and the powerless are those who matter. (Mt 19:13–15)
The first are last and the last first. (Mk 10:31)
The greatest becomes last and the servant of all. (Mk 10:43–44)
Dignity is in serving and not in being served. (Lk 22:24–27)
Anxiety for self-promotion is death and the gift of self is life. (Mk 8:35)

And all this is summarised and fulfilled on the cross on which he who was in the form of God humbled himself and died the death of a slave, turning death into life and shame into glory (Phil 2:6–9, Jn 17:5).

This call of Jesus to conversion was addressed to Jews and Gentiles alike, to all mankind. It was not a call to change religious affiliation as much as it was a challenge to a change of heart. Even though the Kingdom also has a social dimension and is about transforming society by bringing about new brother-sister relationships, no change in relationships is possible without a prior change of attitudes: a change from putting one's own interests first to those of others. We are being reminded daily in our own environment, watching, or even involved in the continual industrial disputes between workers and management, that there is no perfect industrial structure, no perfect system of wage reform, no perfect scheme for social benefits that satisfies everyone. Any new system or structure is workable and acceptable only in so far as it is supported by the good will and the generous attitude of those involved. Similarly in the tragic situation in Northern Ireland. No change, however imaginative, of 'the system' will bear fruit if there is not first of all a conversion of attitudes of the belligerents on both sides by which they appreciate the human qualities and aspirations of each other.

The new scale of values proposed by Jesus for our more harmonious life and growth to wholeness will work only when the offer of new life made to each of us is accepted by the necessary act of 'con-version', by our adopting new attitudes. Systems and structures and institutions and customs only change because people change.

Conversion is, of its nature, personal; but that is not to say it is individualistic. In fact, conversion to the Kingdom Jesus inaugurates is a conversion from a self-orientated life to a community-orientated life.

So the Kingdom also has a social, exterior dimension. This was emphasised by the bishops in the Second Vatican Council:

> 'It has not pleased God to call men to share his life merely as individuals without any mutual bonds. Rather he wills to mould them into a people' (see John 11:52). AG 2 and LG 9.

If people are to live by new values in their relations with others, then this Kingdom Jesus proclaimed appears as a new social and religious order. Jesus was a nonconformist, a sign of contradiction (Lk 2:34), denouncing the enslaving social and religious order of his day. 'You have heard how it was said to our ancestors ... but I say this to you ...' (Mt 5:20–48). As might be expected, such confrontation created a crisis: 'So the people could not agree about him. Some would have liked to arrest him, but no one actually laid hands on him' (Jn 7:43–44, *JB*). 'Then some of the Pharisees said: "This man cannot be from God ..." Others said: "How could a sinner produce signs like this?" And there was disagreement among them' (Jn 9:16, *JB*).

Unity is the goal of the Kingdom, both internal unity (our achieving wholeness/holiness) and our social unity (through right relationships). Unlike, for instance, Hinduism, Christianity does not lead to absorption into God but to the personal fulfilment which God has planned for each of us, which can only be in union with God. The Christian way is the way of individuality—but not of individualism. The unity of the Kingdom is not a static unity but a creative unity, always creating a better future, a source of new energies and possibilities as the parables of the Leaven and the Mustard Seed so well describe.

But for us people who are internally disintegrated and pulled in all directions by conflicting demands and pressures, the path to unity, both internal and collective, is one of pain.

Till the end of time, the fulfilment of God's creative plan—the coming to birth of the Kingdom—will be through confrontation and pain, through letting go and venturing out.

'Up to the present time all of creation groans with pain, like the pain of childbirth. But it is not just creation alone which groans; we who

have the Spirit as the first of God's gifts also
groan within ourselves, as we wait for God to
make us his sons and set our whole being free'.
(Rom 8:22–23)

7. The four eras of the Kingdom

It seems so long ago since Jesus burst into human history with his revolutionary idea of a new age which his Father intends should be the mode of our life today, and so little appears to have happened to bring about any momentous change in the two thousand intervening years, that we can be forgiven for not appreciating that the Christ-time we live in is really a very new as well as the final era. The author of the letter to the Hebrews reminds us: '... he has made his appearance ... now at the end of the last age ...' (9.26, *JB*). To understand this better, we need to put the Christ-event into perspective.

When Paul speaks in his letter to the Ephesians of God's 'secret plan he had already decided to complete by means of Christ' and explains that plan by saying, 'Even before the world was made, God had already chosen us to be his through our union with Christ' (Eph 1:3–10), he is simply pointing out that from the moment of the human person's first appearance on earth—which could have been as long ago as two million years[1]—he was set on a journey towards 'the full stature of Christ'. Within the time span of two million years the arrival of the Christ on the scene a mere two thousand years ago is a very recent event indeed. Why, we may ask, did it not happen sooner? Why has humanity had to wait for at least 1,998,000 years before we could learn what God's plan is for our destiny, or be empowered to make a quantum leap into the new age which heralds its fulfilment? Our first response is surely one of immense gratitude that we ourselves have been chosen to live in the Christ era, the era in which is proclaimed 'his message which is the secret he hid through all past ages from all mankind but has now revealed to his people' (Col 1:26). We can only assume that the human race needed a process of growth in consciousness before it was sufficiently advanced to be able to comprehend and accept the revelation Jesus brought.

We can speak of four major eras in this development of consciousness concerning God's plan for mankind, and of course they cover very recent history—a mere 4,000 years. We can also speak of them as the four eras of the Kingdom, since the Kingdom is the fulfilment of God's plan for mankind which has been unfolding since creation, though explicitly only with the coming of the Christ. It was he, in his account of the final judge-

---

1. The current estimates of palaeontologists range from half a million to four million years.

ment, who refered to 'the Kingdom which has been prepared for you ever since the creation of the world' (Mt 25:34).

We will look at each of these periods in turn. The four are those of the Jewish people, of Jewish Christianity, of European Christianity, and of world Christianity. It will be noticed that three of those periods are related to the history of Christianity. This is not to say that the Kingdom was not evolving in other areas of the world and through other major religions implicitly, but we observe its growth within the Christian tradition which alone gives it explicit expression.

The period of the Jewish people

There was one characteristic by which the Israelites were culturally different from the tribes which surrounded them. Most of the other peoples of the Bible lands, including the great cultures of Egypt, Mesopotamia and Greece, understood their existence in terms of life cycles. As day follows night, so season follows season and generations give way to generations through cycles of birth, growth, decline and death: an endless cycle of events manipulated by various gods. But the Israelites had a different view of life, of history. The extraordinary event whereby, against enormous odds, they were delivered under the leadership of Moses from their life of slavery to the Egyptians caused them to reflect on the hand of God in their history. Unlike the gods of neighbouring civilisations, their Yahweh seemed to be constantly opening new doors to them, leading them to greater and greater self determination and

unification of the tribes that made up their race.
The more they reflected on the events of their history, the more they saw God's hand in them. For
the Israelites, life was not lived in a closed circle but
there was a direction to it. It seemed to be progres-
sing somewhere. At first this consciousness grew as
an oral tradition, passed down by word of mouth
from one generation to the next. Then, after the
Chosen People settled in the Promised Land, this
tradition began to be written down, over a long
period, by a variety of authors in a variety of styles
and often with exaggeration to emphasise some
events as 'miraculous'. This is the collection of writings that today we Christians call the Old Testament.

The Israelites were a people with a past, a history, through which they could see God leading
them. They were a people who had a future. They
looked forward to the moment when God would
send a Messiah among them, though their expectations of the Messiah differed between different
groups, as we saw in Chapter 2.

During the two thousand years of the Israelites'
recorded history—since God promised Abraham 'I
will give you many descendants, and they will become a great nation' (Gen 12:1–2)—God prepared
his people by a process of deeper and deeper understanding of his ways and of his plan for mankind.

Over periods of wandering as nomads to find
their identity, of settling in a land they could call
their own, of choosing to be led by human kings, of
localising God's presence among them in their Temple, of being purified through conquest and exile,

their awareness of God and of their relationship to God was gradually purified. First from an idea of many gods, to the notion that theirs was the supreme God, to an understanding that there is only one God.

Similarly, their moral code became more refined. Let us take just one example: the path from vengeance to forgiveness. We read in Genesis that Lamech boasted to his wives:

> 'I have killed a young man because he struck me. If seven lives are taken to pay for killing Cain, seventy-seven will be taken if anyone kills me'. (4:23–24)

Moses was much more moderate: he proposed a one-for-one vengeance, 'an eye for an eye and a tooth for a tooth' (Ex 21:23–25). As Moses' followers entered the Land of Canaan they became more lenient, at least to those who injured another by accident. They named six 'cities of refuge' none being more than 30 kilometres away from any village. Any Israelite killing someone by accident could run there to be tried. If found innocent, he was protected. As the Israelites grew to understand that their God was a forgiving God, they realised that the same was expected of them. Then the question arose as to how often one was to be expected to forgive. In the time of Jesus it was generally accepted that one should forgive three times. It was this question that Peter put to Jesus, and received the reply: 'seventy times seven': in other words, every time, without limit (Mt 18:21–22).

Until mankind had evolved to a certain point of

consciousness, the revelation of Jesus would have met with complete incomprehension. 'We were slaves of the ruling spirits of the universe before we reached spiritual maturity. But when the right time finally came, God sent his own Son' (Gal 4:3–4). We have to be honest enough to admit that two thousand years on there are very few people on earth today who have really grasped the full impact of Jesus' Good News and are able to live by his values. The vast majority of us are still more akin to Old Testament people in the way in which we relate to God and to each other. The Kingdom has hardly begun to burst forth!

The period of the Jewish Christianity

This is the shortest but by far the most important period: that in which Jesus came among us, both to enlighten us about our glorious destiny and to empower us to break through to a totally new way of life. 'Your hearts and minds must be made completely new, and you must put on the new self, which is created in God's likeness and reveals itself in the true life that is upright and holy' (Eph 4:23–24). How easily we fail to notice and so fail to be inspired by the 'newness' of the life Jesus offers us and the enormity of the transition from the former life to the latter. And as a consequence, we fail to tap the power given us by the Christ to make that leap forward.

Jesus' own audience was made up of Jews, and the band of men he called to further the mission he had received from the Father were Jews too. We have already seen that Jesus, in speaking of the

Kingdom, was speaking of a reality much broader than was understood by his contemporaries: a Kingdom which was not the restoration of Israel but the universal brotherhood of mankind; a Kingdom which was not political but, while being social, was also interior. He did not intend his Kingdom to be a new religion as we understand the great world religions today; nor for the community of his followers to form a religion over against Judaism, as 'Christianity' was soon to become.

Jesus formed a group around him, a community of disciples, who by their way of life and their message were to continue his mission of making the Christ Age a reality. It was as simple as that. They were in fact called 'The Way' and were regarded in the period following Pentecost as yet another sub-group of Jewish life, as were the Pharisees, the Saducees, the Essenes, the Zealots, the Qumran community. Jesus prescribed no new form of worship, so they continued with their Jewish worship, going to the Temple in Jerusalem each day for prayer (Acts 3:1); they observed the Jewish diets (Acts 10:14), and continued to circumcise their sons (Acts 21:21). They did not see themselves as any different from their co-religionists except that they recognised that the promised Messiah had come, a new age had begun: they were fulfilled Jews. So it was that when an angel released the Apostles from jail he instructed them: 'Go and stand in the Temple, and tell the people all about this new life' (Acts 5:20). As the Christian Jews later found themselves among Gentile people, their leaders—the Apostles—began to understand they had a mission beyond Palestine. With the destruction of Jerusalem and the second Temple in AD 70 by the Romans, the followers of 'The Way' fled from their own country and made a cultural leap out of Judaism.

The period of European Christianity

The enormity of this leap taken by the small new Jewish sect, out of Palestine onto the stage of the then known world, is easily overlooked. It had a number of universally important consequences for the next 1,900 years of Christianity.

There was the growing realisation that the 'Second Coming' of the Christ was not as immediate as had been presumed. And as the truth of this dawned upon those early followers, they began to understand themselves as the Body of Christ, the new presence of Christ in the world. As Jesus had made the Kingdom a reality by living as a Kingdom person, so they, as the group formed by Jesus, became identified with the Kingdom. As they called themselves the 'Ekklesia' (Church) to emphasise their break with the synagogue, all that Jesus had said about the Kingdom was interpreted as being said about the Church. And since the loaded Jewish phrase 'Kingdom of God' would have had little meaning to Greek-culture Christians, the expression was rarely used in the speeches and writings of the Apostles.

As the community grew in numbers and in geographical extent, it became institutionalised and began to show the characteristics of a 'religion'. In the first place, it formalised its own way of worship.

With the Temple destroyed, there was no holy place for worship. The simple gathering of followers meeting to break bread together in their homes and celebrate the continuing presence of the Lord in their midst, became a cultic act which included the synagogue liturgy.

Secondly, the simplicity of the announcement of the Good News encountered the Greek world of philosophers, where it became intellectualised. Harnack has summed up this development: 'When the Messiah became Logos the Gospel became theology.' As the message spread, it became necessary to write down different accounts of Jesus' life and teaching to ensure that the true tradition was passed down. We must remember that everything the Apostles preached about Jesus and everything written in the New Testament was written about a Jesus who had risen from the dead and who lives. It was the resurrection that gave meaning to everything Jesus had ever done or said. Their declaration that 'Jesus is Lord' (Acts 2:36) contained not only the whole message of Jesus himself, because it contained the implication that everything he had said must be true, but also that all he had promised would come about is now fulfilled. So they did not present the teaching of Jesus so much as the Jesus who teaches.

Thirdly, organisation became necessary; overseers had to be appointed. What was 'The Way'— the new way of life—became an institution, an elaborate religion, so that 'Christians' became a third people alongside Jews and Pagans, a force to be reckoned with in the Roman Empire. Not only did Kingdom and Church become identified but Kingdom and Empire: the Empire of Christendom. It is said that Charlemagne saw himself as the new David and had his throne in Aachen modelled after the throne of Solomon.

The history of mankind's understanding of Jesus' revelation about the Kingdom is read in the history of the Church, and the history of the Church is read in the political history of Europe.

Having lost sight of her purpose vis-a-vis the Kingdom, the Church exercised her presence in the world in certain ways, which we can now judge from our present-day understanding as being detrimental to rather than supportive of the values of the Kingdom. We can name three such ways in particular. First, there was the presumption that Popes and Bishops should possess a power parallel to, and in some cases even greater than, the temporal rulers in order to fulfil their spiritual office. Pope Innocent II in the 13th century was the most powerful ruler in the whole of Europe. Between the 12th and 17th centuries, most European bishops ruled over large estates, and even over whole regions of a country. Of the eight 'electors' of the Emperor in Germany, four were bishops who had this right because they were rulers of provinces.

A second form of misuse of power, this time spiritual, was the 'force' employed to preserve the supremacy of the Christian faith—the Crusades in order to destroy the Infidel and the Inquisition as a treatment for heretics—and always with such concern for the individual's eternal salvation. Then thirdly, from the 15th century onwards, the Church identified with the morality of the trading or middle classes, a characteristic that can still be noticed today, whether it be in the support of the 'rights' of land owners or corrupt dictators in parts of the developing world, or her dubious speculations on the world financial market.

The present period of world Christianity

Karl Rahner, the well known German theologian, believed that in our century the Church is once again taking a great leap forward in moving out from being a Western-orientated Church to becoming a worldwide multicultural Church: as great a step as it took in moving out of Palestine into the Gentile culture in its early years. This major step is one of the causes of the awakened interest today in the whole concept of the Kingdom as different from and as greater than the Church. We need to devote a whole chapter to this fourth period because of its importance to us as the context of our lives. But before we do this, we must give our attention to the development of the Kingdom-Church relationship.

8. The Church:
Sign of the Kingdom

As we saw in the last chapter, for almost all of the Church's history—from the time of the Apostles right up until recently—the Catholic Church has identified herself with the Kingdom of God on earth.

A new understanding of the Kingdom, and of the Church as being at the service of the Kingdom, has emerged over the last few decades. The reasons for this change of view might be summarised under three headings. First is the contemporary world-wide concern for the future of humanity caused by our growing awareness that the whole of mankind is inextricably bound together in moving forward to one common destiny; an awareness that is born of the ease of immediate communication between all parts of our globe and of our increasing economic interdependence.

Secondly, the Church has found herself growing into a new relationship with the world—the whole world, with its variety of cultures. The last 150 years has seen an unprecedented expansion of her missionary activity which has brought her into dialogue with the other great world religions. This same expansion has exposed the counter witness given by the apparent rivalry between different groups of Christians competing to claim Church members in the name of the same Christ. Pope Paul VI expressed it in these words:

> 'The power of evangelisation will find itself considerably diminished if those who proclaim the Gospel are divided among themselves in all sorts of ways. Is this not perhaps one of the great sicknesses of evangelisation today? Indeed, if the Gospel we proclaim is seen to be rent by doctrinal disputes, ideological polarisations or mutual condemnations among Christians, at the mercy of the latter's differing views on Christ and the Church and even because of their different concepts of society and human institutions, how can those to whom we address our preaching fail to be disturbed, disoriented, even scandalised?' (EN 77)

It is not surprising that the modern ecumenical movement had its origins in inter-denominational missionary congresses early in this century. The Second Vatican Council saw the establishment of three new Vatican secretariats: that for promoting Christian unity, that for non-Christian religions and that for non-believers. It was this Council, too, that declared quite emphatically that Church membership and eternal salvation were two distinct issues,

(GS 22, AG 7.) The last few decades have seen the Church develop a new theology of the human person, understanding her task as being concerned for the development of all people and the *whole* person: full humanisation in unity, is how Pope Paul VI spoke of mankind's salvation (PP 14).

Thirdly, the Church has been reflecting on her own identity. Going back to her biblical origins, she has come to a deeper understanding of her nature and her role in the world. It is her rediscovery of herself as the sign of the Kingdom—or, in the words of Vatican II, as 'a kind of sacrament of intimate union with God and of the unity of all mankind' (LG 1)—that we must explore in this chapter.

Many of us passed through our learning-the-catechism age at a time, previous to the Second Vatican Council, when a Church-orientated theology still pertained. It was Church-orientated because the Kingdom of God was more often spoken of as the Kingdom of Heaven and this was equated with the 'Church Triumphant'. The Church on earth (the Church Militant) was militant against the powers of evil, symbolised by 'the world'. The Church was battling against a corrupt world from which it snatched people for their salvation. Echoing, entirely out of context, the words of the 15th-century Council of Florence,

'No one remaining outside the Catholic Church, not just pagans but also Jews, heretics and schismatics, can become partakers of eternal life but they will go to the everlasting fire that was prepared for the devil and his angels

unless before the end of life they are joined to
the Church',

the Catholic Church saw its task as that of offering salvation, only through Church membership.
Therefore its missionary task was to 'convert'
individuals—as many as possible—and welcome
them into the Church.

As late as 1960 a Congress on World Mission in
Chicago, at which were gathered representatives of
the Protestant Churches, made a similar declaration:

> 'In the days since the war more than one billion
> souls have passed into eternity and more than
> half of these went into the torment of hell fire
> without even hearing of Jesus Christ or why he
> died on the Cross of Calvary.'

For this group, too, 'evangelising' means increasing
Church membership as the only means of salvation.
This concentration on personal salvation makes of
religion a very individualistic affair, and the parish,
with its various activities, is regarded as a spiritual
filling station where a lot of individuals go to be
'topped up' each Sunday. The effect of this understanding of Church life causes parish life to revolve
around the preparation for and administration of
the sacraments, where the priest's role is chiefly
cultic and sacramental, and where the outreach of
the parish is chiefly towards 'the lapsed'.

During the 1930s and 1940s, a shift began to take
place with a swing away from the idea of the Kingdom as an other-worldly reality to an appreciation
that God was obviously active, albeit through the

Church, in secular events, too. This was at a time when the Church was being understood less as an institution—a 'perfect society' as Canon Law then described it—but as the Mystical Body of Christ. A phenomenon of this period was the rise of several lay apostolate movements through which the laity could share in the mission of the Church—provided their activity was strictly under clerical control! The Church started to become involved in a number of secular activities in different countries, but always with the understanding that they were Church-run and parallel to the purely secular: Catholic political parties, Catholic daily newspapers and radio stations, Catholic building societies, Catholic housing associations and credit unions, Catholic Scouts and Guides, etc. Many of these are still with us, particularly the Catholic hospitals and Catholic schools. The Church was emerging from the sanctuary, but only in order to 'Catholicise' the world's institutions.

During the years leading up to Vatican II, the world-Church opposition gave way to an understanding of the role of the Church within and as part of the world; indeed at the centre of the world as leaven in the dough.

The history of humanity is now seen as one—the world is the place of God's action, drawing all things to himself—and not as two parallel histories, the one secular and profane, the other 'salvation history', as it has been called. It is this view of the Church which is found in the documents of the Second Vatican Council and in subsequent documents. From being a sanctuary Church to which people fled from the world in order to find therein their salvation, she is to become again what she was originally intended to be: a sign Church, an announcement by her message and by her communitarian life, of the Kingdom life-style that God offers and desires for all mankind.

'The Church is that segment of the world which reveals the final goal towards which God is working for the whole world',

is a description appearing in a World Council of Churches document (*Church for Others*, p43) which finds its parallel in Vatican II documents:

'For this the Church was founded: that by spreading the Kingdom of Christ everywhere ... she might bring all men to share in Christ's saving redemption.' (AA 2)
'She becomes on earth the initial budding forth of the Kingdom.' (LG 5)
'The Church has a single intention: that God's Kingdom may come.' (GS 45)

and it is the vocation of Christians to be 'artisans of a new humanity' (GS 30).

It is clear that her relationship with the world is quite changed on account of this new understanding of her role in her ministry to the world.

The Church is not the totality of the Kingdom but is at the service of the Kingdom with a mandate to continue Jesus' mission of manifesting the Kingdom. With this perspective we can understand the change in her motivation for mission, from evangelism—drawing people into Church membership—to evangelisation, upon which subject Pope Paul VI wrote one of his greatest documents, the fruit of a world synod of bishops on this very topic, 'Evangelisation in the Modern World' (EN). In it he describes evangelisation as the task of converting cultures to the values of the Gospel,

> 'affecting and as it were upsetting, through the power of the Gospel, mankind's criteria of judgement, determining values, points of interest, lines of thought, sources of inspiration and models of life, which are in contrast with the Word of God and the plan of salvation.'
> (EN 19)

As we have seen, this changed understanding of the world-Church relationship is not confined to the Catholic Church. The World Council of Churches' document already quoted describes the change in these words:

> 'In the past it has been customary to maintain that God is related to the world through the Church. When we sharpen this view into a formula, the sequence would be: God—Church—world. This has been understood to mean that God is primarily related to the Church and only secondarily to the world by means of the Church. Further, it has been held that God relates himself to the world through the Church in order to gather everyone possible from the world into the Church. God, in other words, moves through the Church to the world. We believe that the time has come to question this sequence and to emphasise an alternative.

According to this alternative the last two items in God—Church—world should be reversed, so that it reads instead God—world—Church. That is, God's primary relationship is to the world, and it is the world and not the Church that is the focus of God's plan.' (p16)

Two more quotations from Paul VI leave us in no doubt about the Church's role today:

'While the Church is proclaiming the Kingdom of God and building it up, she is establishing herself in the midst of the world as the sign and instrument of this Kingdom which is and which is to come.' (EN 59)

He shares with us his dream for a witnessing Christian Community, which in its manner of living inevitably causes people to ask: 'What makes it tick?'

'Above all the Gospel must be proclaimed by witness. Take a Christian or a handful of Christians who, in the midst of their own community, show their capacity for understanding and acceptance, their sharing of life and destiny with other people, their solidarity with the efforts of all for whatever is noble and good. Let us suppose that, in addition, they radiate in an altogether simple and unaffected way their faith in values that go beyond current values, and their hope in something that is not seen and that one would not dare to imagine. Through this wordless witness these Christians stir up irresistible questions in the hearts of those who see how they live: Why are they like this? Why do they live in this way? What or who is it that inspires them? Why are they in our midst?' (EN 21)

The change of understanding that has been going on during the last four decades regarding the relationship of the Church to the world, occasioned by a renewed understanding of what Jesus was saying about the Kingdom, can be seen also in the parallel development of understanding of, on the one hand, the reason for mission, and on the other the reason for the Church's concern for social matters and how the two have drawn together. In the pre-1940s, at a time when scholastic theology was dominant, the great motivation for mission outreach (to what were then called the 'foreign missions') was to save souls as individuals, while social work was undertaken because to exercise charity was the work of a good Christian. In the next period, up to the Second Vatican Council, when theology was returning to its biblical roots, the aim of mission to the Third World countries became more community-centred: it was to establish the Church; by which, however, was generally meant to establish a native hierarchy. Social work in the meantime was seen as a more positive contribution to developing countries as a way of inserting spiritual values. Now in the decades following Vatican II, in an era when Liberation Theology has taken the stage in the developing world, the Church understands that her concern must be equally with spiritual and material development—with the development of the whole person—because both are the concern of that Kingdom which God is bringing about beyond the

Church's visible influence, and which the Church has the special task of enunciating by her spoken and by her lived message.

The major divisions that exist between Christians today are less the classical divides between different denominations—whether one is a Methodist or Baptist or Anglican or Roman Catholic—but rather depend upon whether one is a fundamentalist or an ecumenist, a charismatic/pentecostal or a non-charismatic, or whether one's Christian life is Kingdom-orientated or Church-orientated. In fact I believe that this last is even fundamental to the other divisions.

Today there are, among Christians generally, two extreme expressions of the Church-Kingdom relationship. The first, lingering from past times, is in the complete identity of the Church with the Kingdom so that there is still belief in the literal understanding of the motto 'Outside the Church there is no salvation', first coined by Cyprian of Carthage as long ago as the 3rd century. The other is that Jesus never meant to found a Church but that it came into being when the Apostles realised that the second coming of Christ was not imminent. The truth lies between the two: that Jesus did found a community to perpetuate his mission—'I sent them into the world, just as you sent me into the world' (Jn 17:18)—and this community we call 'Church'. But we acknowledge that not all that we include in that word today as pertaining to the Church was instituted by Christ (LG 8).

Let these words from the statement of the Latin American bishops at their conference in Puebla in

1979 summarise what we have been saying:

'The core of Jesus' message is the proclamation of the Kingdom, which is coming and is rendered present in Jesus himself. Though it is not a reality detachable from the Church (LG 8), it transcends the Church's visible bounds (LG 5). For it is to be found in a certain way wherever God is ruling through his grace and love, wherever he is overcoming sin and helping human beings to grow toward the great communion offered them in Christ. This activity of God is also found in the hearts of human beings who live outside the perceptible sphere of the Church (LG 16; GS 22; UR 3). But that definitely does not mean that membership in the Church is a matter of indifference (OAP 1, 8).

Thus the Church received the mission to announce and establish the Kingdom (LG 5) among all peoples. The Church is its sign. In the Church we find the visible manifestation of the project that God is silently carrying out throughout the world. The Church is the place where we find the maximum concentration of the Father's activity. Through the power of the Spirit of Love, the Father is solicitously seeking out human beings to share his own trinitarian life with them—a gesture of ineffable tenderness. The Church is also the instrument that ushers in the Kingdom among human beings in order to spur them on to their definitive goal.

The Church 'becomes on earth the initial

budding forth of that kingdom' (LG 5). Under the influence of the Spirit, that seed is to grow in history until the day when God may be 'all in all' (I Cor 15:28). Until then the Church will remain open to further perfection in many respects and permanently in need of self-evangelisation, greater conversion, and purification (LG 5).

But the Kingdom is already here in the Church. The Church's presence on our continent is Good News because it fully satisfies our people's hopes and aspirations, even if only in a germinal way.

Herein lies the 'mystery' of the Church: it is a human reality made up of limited and impoverished human beings; but it is also suffused with the unfathomable presence and power of the triune God, who in the Church shines forth, calls together, and saves (LG 4, 8; SC 2).

Today's Church is not yet the Church that it is called upon to be. It is important to keep this in mind to avoid a false triumphalistic outlook. On the other hand, too much emphasis should not be placed on its failings, because in it the power that will bring about the definitive Kingdom is already effectively present and at work in the world.'[1]

---

1. *Puebla*, official English translation, paras 226–231, St Paul Publications, Slough, 1980.

(A summary of the shift taking place in our time from a Church-orientated Christianity to a Kingdom-orientated Christianity is provided as Appendix I.)

9. The Kingdom:
Our hope for today

'The final age of the world has already come upon us.' (LG 48)

We traced in Chapter 7 how the development of the concept of God's Kingdom as the expression of God's plan for mankind has passed through three major eras. It is to the fourth and final era of Kingdom realisation that we must now turn our attention: the Kingdom as it touches our present-day lives. There was, in the first period, the development of the idea of God's relationship with man understood by the People of Israel as the special relationship between God and a nation, his People. This led to certain political expectations which proved false. Secondly, there was the historically short but otherwise unique period in which the Kingdom as God's vision for mankind was made explicit and became a reality by the life and teaching of Jesus. Thirdly, with the spread of the Church to Europe and the conversion of the Emperor Constantine, the Church became identified with the Kingdom in the Christendom of the then known world.

Today we are entering the fourth era, where the Kingdom is thought of in the context of the whole world, geographical and cultural, to which the Church is sent as 'the initial budding forth of that Kingdom' (LG 5).

We saw in the last chapter that it is not solely in the Church that God acts but that he is bringing about the fulfilment of his plan for the world directly through all people of goodwill, although the community of Jesus' followers are his specially chosen instrument. In order to 'take its agenda from the world' that community, the Church, has constantly to be reading 'the signs of the times' in the gospel meaning of that expression (Mt 16:1-3): signs of God's action in our history to further his plan.

The Bishops at the Second Vatican Council reminded us:

'The People of God believes that it is led by the Spirit of the Lord, who fills the earth. Motivated by this faith, it labours to decipher authentic signs of God's presence and purpose in the happenings, needs and desires in which this People has a part along with other men of our age. For faith throws a new light on everything, manifests God's design for man's total vocation, and thus directs the mind to solutions which are fully human.' (GS 11)

By exercising this task we can see that at this moment of history there are signs abroad, for those 'with eyes to see and ears to hear', that humanity is on the verge of a great evolutionary step forward into an entirely new era—a new level of consciousness now becoming generally referred to both within and outside the religious tradition as the New Age. This phrase must have significance for Christians who read in the Book of Revelation: 'And now I make all things new' (Rev 21:5), and of whom St Paul said: 'For anyone who is in Christ, there is a new creation; the old creation has gone, and now the new one is here' (2 Cor 5:17, *JB*).

Astrologists who interpret history as unfolding in great 2,000-year strides look forward to the end of this millenium as ushering in the Age of Aquarius, the symbol of which is a man bearing a pitcher of water. Water is used in all the major religions to symbolise the cleansing power of the Spirit. At the end of the Last Supper, during which Jesus had used water to wash his disciples' feet, he promised that at a later time there would be an outpouring of the Spirit to enlighten us with truths that the Apostles were not then able to comprehend: 'I have much more to tell you, but now it would be too much for you to bear. When, however, the Spirit comes, who reveals the truth about God, he will lead you into all the truth ... He will tell you of things to come' (Jn 16:12–13).

This promise is usually related to Pentecost, but it would be naive to think of Pentecost as a one-time event: it was the beginning of an era. There are those who speak of the awakening to a new consciousness of our present day as a New Pentecost. Pope Paul VI wrote in 1975: 'We live in the Church at a privileged moment of the Spirit' (EN 75).

Dare we hope that this new consciousness is awakening mankind at last to an awareness of the deeper meaning of the Good News of Jesus, of how Jesus has offered us a new way of living and relating which is more fully human because through Jesus we have found our entry into the God-life? As long ago as the second century after Christ, Irenaeus wrote: 'Our Lord Jesus Christ did through his transcendent love become what we are, that we might become what he is.' And two centuries later this was more succinctly expressed by Athanasius: 'He was made man, that we might be made God.'

What are the signs around us of this New Age of consciousness, this great leap forward in mankind's evolution to the Age of the Spirit? If the goal of the Kingdom is personal, social and cosmic unity, then we must be looking for signs:

—of growth towards personal integrity;
—of the drawing together of mankind;
—and of mankind's greater harmony with the environment.

We can do no more here than list some of the trends in this direction that we notice in our society, with no pretence that the list is complete. Every reader will be able to add his or her own observations.[1]

---

1. For further reading on the phenomena and trends of our time that point to a break-through into a new age, the following books are recommended: Bühlmann, Walbert: *The Chosen Peoples*, St Paul Publications, Slough, 1982; Bühlmann, Walbert: *The Church of the Future*, St Paul ▷

1. Mankind's growth towards personal integrity

—This century has seen the emergence of the human sciences—anthropology, sociology, psychology, psychiatry—leading to a better understanding of our human evolution, our ways of relating to others and to society and the relationship of body, soul and spirit.

—A growing appreciation of the subjective element in science.

—A more holistic approach to healing. In medicine, appreciating the interplay of body, mind, spirit and environment. In religion, that reconciliation is not simply the concern of the soul but that spiritual healing must be concerned with physical health, memories, our personal history, the stressful environment.

—Humanity's new understanding of itself as the centre of its world. Now that we are able to control our environment on a grand scale (and endeavour-

▷ Publications, Slough, 1986; Capra, Fritjof: *The Turning Point*, Flamingo, Fontana Paperbacks, London, 1983; Ferguson, Marilyn: *The Aquarian Conspiracy*, Paladin Book, Granada, London, 1982; Happold, FC: *Religious Faith and Twentieth Century Man*, Darton, Longman and Todd, London, 1980; Myers, Norman (Ed): *The Gaia Atlas of Planet Management*, Pan Books, London, 1985; Russell, Peter: *The Awakening Earth*, Routledge and Kegan Paul, London, 1982; Spink, Peter: *Spiritual Man in a New Age*, Darton, Longman and Todd, London, 1980; Spink, Peter: *The End of an Age*, Omega Trust Publications, Tunbridge Wells, 1983; Toffler, Alvin: *The Third Wave*, Pan Books, London, 1981.

ing to control outer space) we are less dependent on nature.

—Before, we could only survive in a hostile world by surrendering to a pattern of customs, taboos and ethical parameters. Now we feel free to challenge all previous notions, beliefs and codes of behaviour.

—We are less concerned with the influence of the past: more with shaping our future, which we feel we have the power to do.

—The emergence of so many nations over the last three decades, in Africa especially, from colonial government to self rule.

—A growing desire for participation, whether in politics, industry or Church. Individuals are less content to be swept along either by social convention or by the powerful few. They desire to have a say in shaping their own and their family's future.

—The increasing manifestation, in different forms, of 'People Power'.

—This is partly due to an accelerated growth in education: greater availability of education and of almost unlimited information through computers.

—A complementary desire for spiritual experience, an experience of God and a search for Truth rather than truths. The growing popularity of methods of contemplative meditation.

—A diminishing of the unique esteem given to rationalism but a development of the left, intuitive brain and a greater respect for creativity.

—A world-wide aspiration, among the young especially, for authenticity.

2. The drawing together of mankind

—Advances in communications media give us an instant awareness of and involvement in world affairs. We have a sense of belonging to a 'global village'. By pressing a few buttons on our telephone we can speak to a friend in almost any country in the world.

—Increased ease and frequency of travel opens up new horizons and an appreciation of other cultures.

—Our pluralistic societies give us an experience of what were once 'foreign' cultures and creeds.

—Our home environment becoming increasingly multiracial.

—A decline of nationalism and of the ability of each nation to determine its own life in isolation, irrespective of others, eg involvement in such groupings as the EEC.

—A greater tolerance of and dialogue with peoples with different ideologies.

—Awareness of the North-South divide, and more appreciation of the interdependence of all peoples of the earth.

—A concern for the needs of the whole of humanity—eg, immediate response to appeals for help in times of natural calamities.

—The setting-up of world and continental bodies as instruments of unity: UN, OAU, etc; and the organisations for particular concerns: FAO, UNESCO, UN High Commission for Refugees, The World Bank, International Monetry Fund, etc.

—Nearer home, organisations for world charity: CAFOD, Christian Aid, and their equivalents in many other countries.

—A worldwide aspiration to achieve equality, expressed in different political philosophies.

—A growing awareness of the need for equal rights for men and women.

—Signs of more caring for and sharing with the marginalised peoples by such campaigns as the Year for the Disabled, International Youth Year, etc.

—The worldwide phenomenon, both inside the Church and in secular society, of the search for new forms of community living: for structures that allow people to relate at a more human and deeper level through small groupings.

—Within the Church, a shift in the 1970s from a Western-centred Church to a Church whose centre of balance is now in the Third World, in the Southern Hemisphere, with the consequent openness to pluriformity in place of uniformity. The recognition that we are in the age of the World Church.

—The rise of ecumenical dialogue between different Christian denominations and the search for a way forward to some form of unity. A similar opening of dialogue between the major religions of the world.

—A new awareness of our unity in cosmic consciousness; of our oneness in the cosmic mind.

3. Mankind's greater harmony with the environment

—A greater concern to be in harmony with, rather than to use (and abuse), creation. Understanding that we are less owner of than partner with nature.

—The rise of environmental studies and the emergence of conservationists, environmentalists and ecologists: Greenpeace.

—The entry of this concern into the arena of politics: the Green Party.

—The fear of nuclear disaster and the campaigns against the production of nuclear power.

—The return to more natural power sources: solar, tide and wind energy. The development of alternative technology.

—A growing trend to move out of conurbations and return to rural living—to be in contact with the soil.

—A search for more simple, and more fully human, lifestyles.

—A recognition of the body's inability to adapt to the increasing acceleration of change, that the tempo of life is damaging to inner harmony.

—Concern for population growth vis-a-vis world food production and distribution.

—A growing realisation that the biggest is not necessarily the best: that devolution is often more human and therefore more productive.

But, one might ask, if these trends in our society are to be interpreted positively as signs of mankind's break through into a new age, a step towards the accomplishment of the Kingdom of God, how is one to understand the evident and, it seems, increasing evils and fragmentations that seem equally to be characteristic of our time?

It is a mark of every major cultural transition that the more a new culture emerges, the declining culture exhibits conflicting values to an increasingly pronounced degree. The anthropologist Mircea Eliade demonstrated how cultures undergo a series of regressions to the state of chaos before the emergence of a new stage of creativity. Sociologists explain the phenomenon as a polarisation.

Just as we have spoken of personal, social and cosmic signs of hope, so we must recognise signs of personal, social and cosmic evil. We are not simply faced with greater personal evil, nor even with greater collective personal evil, such as the eroding of the family unit or the rise in local crime and violence, that might be attributed to a breakdown of our traditional (Christian, in the case of the Western world) moral standards. We are faced with evil on a global scale which seems to be beyond human control. It is the evil of the system, the evil of the culture. This is manifest in the evils which are no longer confined to a single continent: the many forms of racial hatred; the crimes committed in the name of national security, whatever be the ideology such security is said to defend; the seemingly irreversible stockpiling of nuclear missiles threatening a worldwide holocaust; the hijacking, bomb-planting and terrorist attacks related to grievances in other countries and even other continents; the pollution of the atmosphere and rape of the environment in the interests of profit on a world scale; the monopoly of power of multinational corporations controlling the economic lives of tens of millions of people all around the globe; the widening gap between rich and poor, between the Northern and Southern hemispheres.

These are symptoms of the death struggle of a disappearing value-system becoming more and more entrenched when challenged by the rising confidence of a new creative minority. What is happening in this struggle, beneath the surface, is very well described by Fritjof Capra in his book *The Turning Point* (P 466).

Such polarisation can be compared with the effect upon the sea's surface when, after an oil spill, a form of detergent is spread on the water. The detergent brings about a separation of the clear water from the polluted by causing the oil to coagulate and become more concentrated. It is doubtful if there is any greater degree of evil per capita in our world than there ever was, but it is the more vicious for being more concentrated.

Our news media do not help us to obtain a balanced view of our world: all the good that is being done does not make 'news'. Perhaps it says a lot for our innate goodness, or at least for our expectation of goodness, that what makes 'news' is the very opposite: crime, disaster, accidents, coups, violence.

We who are Christians and have been given the revelation of the secret of God's plan for mankind (Col 1:25–27) are required to be proclaimers of good news, to be beacons of hope in a world which is suffering particularly from a lack of hope, from a despair about our future. The world's bishops at the Second Vatican Council a couple of decades ago, echoing the words of Teilhard de Chardin, declared:

'The future of humanity lies in the hands of those who are strong enough to provide coming generations with reasons for living and hoping'. (GS 31)

We Christians are a minority in the world, indeed a dwindling minority, but no matter. It has been proved by a theory that goes by different names (Morphic Resonance, Formative Causation) that when only a small percentage makes a breakthrough in consciousness this empowers the whole of mankind to make the same breakthrough.[2]

The new 'rulers' of the earth, those who will determine its future, are not going to be the politically or economically powerful, but the thousands of unknown, hidden, intuitive persons who live with a new consciousness springing from an inner conviction informed by their faith and their trust in the inevitability of the fulfilment of God's plan for mankind. Jesus did promise that it is the meek who will inherit the earth (Mt 5:5).

2. For further reading on this theory the following books are recommended: Russell, Peter: *The Awakening Earth*, Routledge and Kegan Paul, London, 1982; Sheldrake, Rupert: *A New Science of Life*, Paladin Book, Granada, London, 1983.

10. The Parish: A witnessing community of the Kingdom

In this last chapter we need to consider how we, as Christians, bearers to the world of the Good News of Jesus the Christ, can in practice be instruments of ushering in this new and final age of the Kingdom of God. Why should we suppose that we should exercise this in the context of the parish? First, because I believe it is from within the Christian tradition, rather than from outside it, that the seed of the future age of humanity, planted from the moment of mankind's first appearance on earth, made fruitful by Jesus, will reach its fullness. The Christian community, not as a collection of individuals but as that community which is the Body of Christ, is called to be the visible presence of Christ in the world today, the visible presence of the Messiah for our age. Secondly, whatever we may think of the parish as it is constituted today, and whatever way we may believe it has to change in structure to accommodate to our needs tomorrow, we have to recognise that it provides the setting in which the majority of committed Catholics experience their Christian life and find the support of a faith community. Thirdly, for all its defects it is the grouping in which the world witnesses Christian life being lived and shared: it is, or should be, the city on the hilltop (Mt 5:14–16), able to be seen by all the neighbourhood as the embodiment of the Christ's Good News.

The parish is therefore that setting in which the characteristics of the Kingdom should be most consciously promoted. In this chapter we will try to sum up what we have said of the nature of the Kingdom under five headings, representing five of its facets, no single one of which gives a complete picture, each requiring to be complemented by the others. We will relate each to ways in which they might be developed within the context of the present parish.

The Kingdom means new relationships

Jesus introduced us to a new relationship with God as that of son to a father (Rom 8:15) and consequently of men and women to each other as brothers and sisters (Rom 8:29). Only Jesus is the rightful Son of God (Mt 17:5; Jn 3:16), but he offers us an adopted sonship (Jn 1:12–13; Eph 1:5). Being an offer, it requires to be freely accepted by us (Rom 8:12–15; Eph 4:24) through conversion and commitment. So the Kingdom begins to be present among those who freely accept this new relationship. We make this effective by acting upon the understanding that our primary relationship to each other, quite independently of the roles we play or offices we hold in the parish organisation, is that of brother and sister. Irrespective of whether we are cleric or lay, child or parent, choirmaster or cleaner, there exists an interdependence between us as members of the same faith community, all with the task to build up the body of Christ (Eph 4:12). The relationship, for instance, of priest to parishioner is only that of roles and is therefore secondary to their relationship as brother and sister of Christ. We are not divided into givers and receivers. There is none so poor that he has nothing to give: there is none so rich that he has nothing to receive. We each have our individuality and that is unique. It is God's gift to us; it is our gift to others. 'Each one of us has received a special gift in proportion to what Christ has given' (Eph 4:7). The parish should be the first place in which this Christian manner of relating should be evident.

The Kingdom means total liberation

Jesus denounced the enslaving social and religious order of his day. He subordinated the 'Law and the Prophets', which was the dogma of the Old Testament, to the demands of love. Despite the Old Testament prescription 'Do not add anything to what I command you, and do not take anything away' (Deut 4:2), Jesus modified the Law: observance of the Sabbath (Ezek 20:12; Mk 2:27); punishment for adultery (Jn 8:11); divorce (Mk 10:9); legal purification (Mk 7:15); love of friends and enemies (Mt 5:44). To the alarm of the Pharisees, he showed solidarity with the marginalised who did not know the Law (Jn 7:49); he became the voice of those without a voice in society (Mt 11:19); he did not recognise prescribed social divisions (Mk 2:15–17; Lk 9:46); he changed the relationship of master and slave into mutual fraternal service (Mt 23:8–10; Mk 10:42). So in writing to the Galatians Paul speaks of the Kingdom of God as the new order in which 'there is no difference between Jews and Gentiles, between slaves and free men, between men and women' (Gal 3:28).

As Catholics we have not in the past been famous for providing the circumstances for people to grow with 'the glorious freedom of the children of God' (Rom 8:21). On the contrary, the Fall-Redemption framework of our theology has more often concentrated on our sinfulness and bred a sense of guilt and fear. This still lingers in the minds of so many faithful people in our parishes and may even today be the primary reason why not a few attend Mass each Sunday.

An over-emphasis on mankind's fall from grace and the need to be restored in our relationship with God misses the point of what is so new about Jesus' announcement of the Kingdom. The Kingdom is not in the first place about obedience but about creativity: not about restoration to a former primitive state from which mankind fell but about co-operation with God in the creative act of unification at a much higher level.

The Good News challenges us to a fundamental change in our life, from self-centredness to Other-centredness, and such a conversion is achieved only through wrenching ourselves painfully away from self. This is easy for no one, and it is a lifelong process, but the challenge is nevertheless Good News because ultimately it brings about our liberation. But is the Gospel challenge always presented and heard as *good* news in our parishes?

The Kingdom means fullness of life

It is curious that while Matthew, Mark and Luke have Jesus speak of the Kingdom 91 times, John in his Gospel mentions it only twice (Jn 3:3, 5), but expresses the same theme with a different word: Life. The words 'eternal life' occur 19 times and 'life', apparently with exactly the same meaning, 17 times. While on two occasions it has a reference to life after death, on the others he is speaking of a quality of life available already now. Our fullness of life can only be found in our complete orientation towards God's evolving plan for mankind (God's will) in all its aspects: spiritual, communitarian, social, economic; indeed in our becoming attuned to, and living in harmony with, the whole cosmic plan of God.

For Jesus, the coming of the Kingdom is synonymous with the accomplishment of the will of God (Mt 6:10), which is not surprising when we consider that God's will is that which is best for us; or in other words, it is what we desire for ourselves when we desire what is best for ourselves. So St Irenaeus could say: 'The glory of God is the glory of man fully alive.' Participation in God's life is the fulfilment of human society, as it is the fulfilment of each individual.

Are the relationships within our parish com-

munity supportive and life-giving? Are our parish
concerns so concentrated on the liturgical and sacramental life that our concern for the development
of the totality of life is obscured?

The Kingdom means communion of people

This is not a satisfactory heading. 'Community'
would be better, but that word is used to cover such
a range of groups, with varying degrees of unity,
that its full impact is being diminished. God's purpose in the Old Testament was precisely to bring
unity to the Hebrew tribes so that they would become 'a people'. In fact, under God's kingship they
were to become his people (Ez 36:24–28). In the
New Covenant terms, Peter addressed his first letter
'to God's chosen people' and reminded them that
now:

> 'You are the chosen race, the King's priests,
> the holy nation, God's own people, chosen to
> proclaim the wonderful acts of God, who called
> you out of darkness into his own marvellous
> light. At one time you were not God's people,
> but now you are his people ...' (1 Pet 2:9–10)

As God chose the Hebrews as his special people, not
just for their own benefit but to be an instrument of
salvation for all, so Peter reminds those called to be
the Christian chosen people that their election contains a duty of proclamation. They will proclaim
God's wonderful acts precisely by giving witness of
their unity as a people. We can say that unity is the
one quality above all others by which Jesus hoped
his followers would be recognised. It was his final

and deepest wish—his Last Will—expressed in his prayer at the Last Supper for all who would become believers:

> 'I pray that they may all be one, Father! May they be in us, just as you are in me and I am in you. May they be one, so that the world will believe that you sent me.' (Jn 17:21) '. . . so that they may be completely one in order that the world may know that you sent me and that you love them as you love me.' (Jn 17:23)

Evidence of the unity that exists among believers is a necessary channel for our encountering the saving message of Christ, for salvation comes through fraternity. The 'sacrament of fraternity' is the principal sacrament of salvation (Mt 25:31–46; Lk 10:29–37). At a time when 'the world ceases to be a place of brotherhood' (GS 37) Christians must proclaim a clear vision and give 'assurance that the way of love lies open to all men and the effort to establish a universal brotherhood is not a hopeless one' (GS 38).

One of the 'signs of the times' today is people's desire for community. This can only be effected when we are enabled to relate to others in communities which are small enough to experience what it means to be and to be known as a 'person', in the fullness of that word. To meet this need, large anonymous parishes have to reconstitute themselves into communions of basic communities such that the members of each can share together their deepest spiritual experiences—that which gives meaning to the exterior practice of their faith. Only in this way can the right environment for true personal growth be provided by the Church.

The Kingdom is also the Kingdom within

The outer manifestation of the Kingdom, the sociological aspect of the Kingdom of God, is complemented, and indeed brought about, by the growth of the Kingdom within each person. That is, the inner experience of being taken over by God. Paul tells us:

> 'Your hearts and minds must be made completely new, and you must put on the new self, which is created in God's likeness and reveals itself in the true life that is upright and holy.'
> (Eph 4:23–24)

A phenomenon of our present times is the number of people who are seeking a deep and authentic spiritual experience; that which gives meaning, gives soul, to their religious practice. There is the danger that the Church in its parish life is so 'busy' with all the outward manifestations of the Kingdom—worship, education, social concerns—that the most important work of all, that of putting people in direct contact with God, is neglected.

We can be so occupied with teaching truths *about* God that we fail to put people in contact with Truth itself, 'the truth that is in Jesus' (Eph 4:21). We can concentrate all our effort into the outward observances but fail to feed people's hunger to experience God with that inner, intuitive knowledge which is cultivated most easily by the practice of contemplative meditation. This is the deeper prayer life that people are seeking today, even many of those who are only on the fringe of parish life, who no longer, perhaps, find what they most long for in the plethora of parish *activities*.

Unless as much attention is given in our ministering to one another to the growth of the Kingdom 'within' as we give to the Kingdom 'among' us, the latter will simply not become a reality. Everyone who ministers to others in any form in the parish should pray with St Paul:

> 'We ask God to fill you with the knowledge of his will, with all the wisdom and understanding that his Spirit gives. Then you will be able to live as the Lord wants and will always do what pleases him. Your lives will produce all kinds of good deeds, and you will grow in your knowledge of God.
>
> 'May you be made strong with all the strength which comes from his glorious power, so that you may be able to endure everything with patience. And with joy give thanks to the Father, who has made you fit to have your share of what God has reserved for his people in the kingdom of light.' (Col 1:9–12)

Epilogue

It would be fitting to end this modest work with the following quotation from the Bishops at the Second Vatican Council which has inspired it:

'Christ is now at work in the hearts of men through the energy of his Spirit. He arouses not only a desire for the age to come, but, by that very fact, he animates, purifies, and strengthens those noble longings too by which the human family strives to make its life more human and to render the whole earth submissive to this goal.

'We do not know the time for the consummation of the earth and of humanity. Nor do we know how all things will be transformed. As deformed by sin, the shape of this world will pass away. But we are taught that God is preparing a new dwelling place and a new earth where justice will abide, and whose blessedness will answer and surpass all the longings for peace which spring up in the human heart.

'Then, with death overcome, the sons of

God will be raised up in Christ. What was sown in weakness and corruption will be clothed with incorruptibility. While charity and its fruits endure, all that creation which God made on man's account will be unchained from the bondage of vanity.

'Therefore, while we are warned that it profits a man nothing if he gain the whole world and lose himself, the expectation of a new earth must not weaken but rather stimulate our concern for cultivating this one. For here grows the body of a new human family, a body which even now is able to give some kind of foreshadowing of the new age.

'Earthly progress must be carefully distinguished from the growth of Christ's kingdom. Nevertheless, to the extent that the former can contribute to the better ordering of human society, it is of vital concern to the kingdom of God.

For after we have obeyed the Lord, and in his Spirit nurtured on earth the values of human dignity, brotherhood and freedom, and indeed all the good fruits of our nature and enterprise, we will find them again, but freed of stain, burnished and transfigured. This will be so when Christ hands over to the Father a kingdom eternal and universal: "a kingdom of truth and life, of holiness and grace, of justice, love, and peace". On this earth that kingdom is already present in mystery. When the Lord returns, it will be brought into full flower.' (GS 38, 39)

Appendix 1.
Summary of the shift taking place from a Church-orientated Christianity to a Kingdom-orientated Christianity

The three periods are no more than indicative of where the stress was at the time. A development of thought necessarily co-exists with previous thinking.

1930s and 1940s	1950s and 1960s	1970s and 1980s
(Pre-Vatican II thinking predominates)	*(The transitional period leading up to Vatican II)*	*(The development of Vatican II thinking)*
The Church is a perfect society, parallel with human society. The Church is the mystical Body of Christ.	The Church is the sign and sacrament of intimate union with God and of the unity of all mankind. (LG 1)	The Church is the expression on earth—the sign or witness—of what it means to live by Kingdom values. (AA 2, LG 5, GS 45)
The Church's concern with man is split between his body and his soul—chiefly the latter. (Based on Scholastic Theology)	The Church is concerned with the whole man (PP 14) (Based on a return to Biblical Theology).	The Church is concerned with what man can become. (With the insight of Liberation Theology).
The orientation of spirituality is towards man's Fall and Redemption and the evil in man.	'Men ... are the artisans of a new humanity.' (GS 30)	Orientation of spirituality returns to Creation and the power of good in man.

1930s and 1940s	1950s and 1960s	1970s and 1980s
The ethic of obedience: to laws and directives of Church authorities.	Conscience rediscovered as the ultimate norm of personal morality. 'Conscience is the most secret core and sanctuary of a man . . . . according to it he will be judged.' (GS 16)	The ethic of conscience: 'The truth cannot impose itself except by virtue of its own truth.' (DH 1)
The good Christian exercises social charity.	Social work promotes spiritual values.	The Church's concern is equally with spiritual and material matters, as both are the concerns of the Kingdom.
The Church is hierarchical in structure. Members relate according to their authority roles.	The Church is the (New) People of God.	The Church is communitarian in structure. The fundamental relationship of all Christians is that of brother and sister of Jesus Christ, children of the same Father. All those who consciously or unconsciously promote the Kingdom are the New People of God: they may be Church members or they may not.
The Roman Catholic Church is the only true Church.	'The unique Church of Christ which in the Creed we avow as one, holy, catholic and apostolic ... subsists in the (Roman) Catholic Church'. (LG 8)	'The Spirit of Christ does not refrain from using (separated Churches) as means of salvation.' (UR 3)

1930s and 1940s	1950s and 1960s	1970s and 1980s
The purpose of the 'foreign missions' is to save individual souls by baptising pagans into Church membership.	The purpose of missionary activity is to establish the Church—principally the hierarchy—in mission lands. (AG 6)	The Church's mission is the cross-cultural proclamation of the Good News of the Kingdom of God.
The ordinary means of salvation is through Church membership.	The Church is God's chosen but not unique channel of salvation. (GS 22)	Church membership is the extra-ordinary means of salvation for a minority of people.
The Church's (Western) theology, liturgy and structures need some adaptation to other cultures.	'Whatever truth and grace are to be found among the nations are a sort of secret presence of God.' (AG 9)	The Church is called to evangelise culture and cultures (EN 20). The Good News of the Kingdom must be incarnated in all cultures.
Non-Christian religions are evil: they are the subject of conversion.	'The Catholic Church rejects nothing which is true and holy in these religions.' (NA 2) The Holy Spirit is active outside the Church.	Our Christian understanding of the Good News can be enriched by the insights of other religions, (EN 53) in which we discern the presence of the Spirit.
The Kingdom is identified with the Church Triumphant at the end of time.	The Church 'becomes on earth the initial budding forth of that Kingdom.... The Church strains toward the consummation of the Kingdom.' (LG 5)	'Only the Kingdom is absolute.' (EN 8) The Church is relative to the Kingdom.

Appendix 2.
Discussion questions

The following are questions that may well arise in the mind of the reader, with a desire to pursue them further. Their formulation here will facilitate such an exploration by, for example, parish or college discussion groups.

1. Today, the percentage of Christians in the world is diminishing. What does this fact say to us about the outcome of God's plan for the world?

2. Does the Church preach the Gospel in order to make more Christians or in order to change the world?

3. Pope Paul VI said in his Apostolic Exhortation on Evangelisation: 'Only the Kingdom is absolute, and it makes everything else relative'. (EN 8) Is the Church to be counted as part of the absolute or among the relative?

4. If members of other religions can attain holiness not merely despite their religion but through their religion, then for what reason

should we invite them to become Christians?

5. Does the presentation of the gospel message as people hear it today, both within and outside our churches, come across as 'Good News'?

6. In what practical ways can our parish manifest the five characteristics of the Kingdom as given in Chapter 10?

7. Looking at the three periods of development of Church thinking, as presented in Appendix 1, at which stage would be the majority of Catholics today in our country; in our parish?

Acknowledgements

Cover photograph © Associated Newspapers Group plc, Carmelite House, London, EC4Y OJA.

Material from *The Documents of Vatican II*, general editor Walter M Abbott SJ, is published by permission of Geoffrey Chapman, a division of Cassell Ltd.

Unless otherwise stated, all Scripture quotations are from *The Good News Bible* © American Bible Society 1976, published by The Bible Societies and Collins. Used by permission.

Quotations from the *Jerusalem Bible*, published and copyright 1966, 1967 and 1968 by Darton, Longman and Todd Ltd and Doubleday & Co Inc, are used by permission of the publishers.

The Apostolic Exhortation *Evangelii Nuntiandi* of Pope Paul VI is published by the Catholic Truth Society, London, under the title 'Evangelisation in the Modern World' (S 312).

Paragraphs from *The Church for Others* are reproduced by permission of the World Council of Churches.

Quotations from *Puebla*, National Conference of Catholic Bishops, Washington DC, 1979, St Paul Publications/CIIR 1980, paragraphs 226–231, are used by permission.